BIRDING
with Bill Oddie

BIRDING
with Bill Oddie

Bill Oddie and Stephen Moss

Approved by the RSPB
BBC BOOKS

This book was first published in 1997 to accompany the television series
entitled *Birding with Bill Oddie* which was first broadcast in 1997.
The series was produced by BBC Education for Adults.
Executive Producer: Fiona Pitcher
Producer: Stephen Moss

This paperback edition published in 2011 by BBC Books,
an imprint of Ebury Publishing. A Random House Group company.

The Random House Group Limited Reg. No. 954009

Addresses for companies within the Random House Group can be found at
www.randomhouse.co.uk

A CIP catalogue record for this book is available from the British Library.

ISBN 978 1849903080

The Random House Group Limited supports the Forest Stewardship Council (FSC), the
Leading international forest certification organization. All our titles that are printed on
Greenpeace approved FSC certified paper carry the FSC logo. Our paper procurement policy
can be found at www.randomhouse.co.uk/environment

Designed by Judith Robertson
Illustrations by Bill Oddie

Printed and bound in Germany by Firmengruppe Appl, Wemding.

To buy books by your favourite authors and register for offers,
visit www.eburypublishing.co.uk

Picture Credits

BBC pages 9 (Mark Carey) and 17; DAVID M. COTTRIDGE pages 56, 92 and 129;
PHOTOLIBRARY pages 21 (Hans Reinhard/Okapia), 80-1 (Bridget Wheeler) and 84 (Carlos
Sanchez); PHOTOSHOT pages 17 (Westend61), 20 (Mike McKavett), 25 (Felix Labhardt), 33
(Eero Murtomaki), 41 (Stephen Dalton), 44 (Gordon Langsbury), 45 (Dennis Green), 57 (Dennis
Green), 60-1 (Dennis Green), 65 (George McCarthy), 68-9 (Kim Taylor), 72-3 (E.A. Janes), 85
(Hans Reinhard), 101 (Gordon Langsbury), 125 (Melvin Grey), 156 (Rod Williams), 164-5 (Paul
van Gaalen), 192 (Paul Meitz), 212 (Wayne Lankinen) and 213 top (Stephen J. Krasemann);
RSPB-images.com pages 24 (W.S.Paton), 36 (Mark Hamblin), 37 (Mark Hamblin) and 173 (Steve
Knoll); GLYN SATTERLEY page 176-7; M.C. WILKES page 149; STEVE YOUNG page 96-7.

CONTENTS

ABOUT THE AUTHORS

Bill Oddie is, without doubt, Britain's best-known birdwatcher – or birder, as this growing tribe of enthusiasts is now generally known. His passion for birds goes back to his childhood. Like most kids in those days, he spent some time as a delinquent egg collector, before picking up a pair of binoculars and pursuing birds in a more constructive manner.

Bill has travelled throughout Britain and the world in search of birds; and in the past two decades has passed on his passion, knowledge and boundless enthusiasm through television series such as Springwatch, Autumnwatch, How to Watch Wildlife, Bill Oddie Goes Wild, and the series which this book originally accompanied, Birding with Bill Oddie. If anyone is responsible for the huge birding boom during the past few years, it is undoubtedly him. This has also led to a growing interest in, and concern for, Britain's wild creatures and the places where they live. For which both the British public – and the wildlife – can only say a huge thank you Bill!

Stephen Moss is the man behind the TV series mentioned above. He too has been watching birds since he was a child, and has had the good fortune to travel to all the world's seven continents in search of wildlife; sometimes with a film crew and Bill in tow, at other times purely for pleasure. Like Bill, he loves communicating his passion for birds and wildlife to others, which he also does through his many books, articles and radio series.

Stephen has spent his entire working life at the BBC, including the past 14 years at the Natural History Unit in Bristol. Now, after almost 30 years, he is leaving to pursue new challenges; including, he hopes, spending more time watching birds.

Bill and Stephen first met at Stodmarsh in May 1975, when Stephen saw a very rare Little Bittern (and Bill, unfortunately, didn't). They met again in 1983, and Bill suggested that they make a TV series together. 13 years later, in 1996, they finally did: Birding with Bill Oddie. In the following decade they made a dozen series and almost 100 programmes, travelling throughout Britain and to locations across the globe. They worked with some remarkable people, saw some amazing birds, and had some unforgettable times. They remain great friends to this day.

PREFACE BY BILL ODDIE

A few years ago, I saw an advert for an American book called *The Joy of Birding*. I never could find the book, but I really like that title. It set me thinking just how many joys there are. It could be seeing just one bird, a particular rarity perhaps. Or it could be the thrill of incredible numbers of birds. Or witnessing an impressive migratory movement. Or getting a memorable view of an especially beautiful bird. Or observing a fascinating piece of behaviour – maybe an elaborate display or a hunting pass. Or it could be some wild and wonderful place where birdwatching takes you. Or the novelty of seeing an unexpected bird in an incongruous setting. Or perhaps it's the people you meet. Or the other interests that birdwatching leads you to – maybe drawing, or painting, or photography.

This book is intended to help you discover the joy of birding. It is not strictly speaking 'the book of the series'. It couldn't be, since due to the schedules of publishing it has to be written before we start filming! It is even impossible to anticipate what exactly will be in the series. That is another of the joys: unpredictability. However, what Stephen Moss and I hope we can achieve, both in these pages and on the screen, has a dual purpose. First, to introduce you to some of the principles and techniques that will either help start you birding or add to what you already know. Second, to capture the feeling of what it is like to be actually out there 'in the field'. Call it theory and practice, if you like. A two-in-one offer!

Since Stephen is a producer, and therefore more organized than me, I am leaving most of the instructional stuff to him. I, on the other hand, am older, and therefore have a longer memory, so I will be telling the stories. I have been birding most of my life. I could write several books about it – in fact I have! – but for this one I have restricted myself to four pieces that I hope capture some of the essential ingredients of this ever-fascinating hobby and demonstrate how the principles apply to the real thing.

One thing Stephen and I coincide on. We both feel strongly that there is a great deal more to birding than simply identifying species and ticking them off a list. That is the beginning, certainly, and it is part of the satisfaction, but there is so much more besides. The places, the experiences, the feelings, the fun, even the frustrations. These are the joys. This is what turns us on. Whether or not we can convey this to you remains to be seen. If we spot you out there with your binoculars, we'll know we've done it. Enjoy.

SECTION 1:
THE THEORY

1 GETTING STARTED

WHY WATCH BIRDS?

The observation of birds may be a superstition,
a tradition, an art, a science, a pleasure, a hobby, or a bore;
this depends entirely on the nature of the observer.
James Fisher, *Watching Birds* (1941)

Birdwatching is one of Britain's fastest-growing and most popular leisure activities, enjoyed by people from all walks of life. Why? Perhaps because birds are the most familiar and noticeable of all living creatures. They're widespread, relatively easy to observe and endlessly fascinating: once you start watching them it's hard to stop. Birdwatching also gives you the chance to find out more about the living world, while enjoying your leisure time in a creative and fulfilling way. This may be either solo or in company, or perhaps as a shared family activity – children will need little encouragement to become absorbed.

At some point, every birdwatcher is asked the same question: why do you watch birds? Answering the question, without stating the obvious, isn't easy. Here are some very good reasons for watching birds.

- It gets you out in the open air – to places you wouldn't otherwise visit.
- It's a challenge – birds are sometimes hard to see, and often difficult to identify.
- When you watch birds, and the way they behave, you're getting a privileged insight into their daily lives.
- You can watch birds anywhere – from the centre of the city to a remote offshore island.
- Birding is a social activity, but when you're tired of other people, you can still do it on your own!

Bill enjoying a quiet moment's birding – by the sewage outfall at Inverness!

• The more we know about birds, the easier it is to conserve them and their habitats – which will ultimately benefit ourselves and future generations.

WHO WATCHES BIRDS?

Until a few years ago, the stereotypical image of the birdwatcher was of a retired colonel or spinster headmistress peering myopically at a bush through antique opera-glasses. Then, almost overnight, the image changed. Tabloid newspapers started writing about the 'twitcher': a kind of ornithological obsessive whose main purpose in life was to pursue rare birds (see page 96).

The truth, of course, is rather less exciting. Birdwatchers come in all shapes and sizes: young and old, from all over the country, and from very varied social backgrounds. Increasing numbers of people have a casual interest in birds, perhaps waiting for the impulse to take up birdwatching, but not sure where to start.

Birding with Bill Oddie will guide you through the 'fieldcraft' of birdwatching, enabling you to find, observe and learn about birds for yourself. It will open your eyes to the passion, the thrills, the disasters, the humour and, above all, the sheer enjoyment of birdwatching.

SO YOU WANT TO BECOME A BIRDWATCHER?

You didn't realize this was happening at first. Perhaps it began when you first noticed the birds in your garden or the local park. Or maybe someone gave you a bird book for Christmas. Then one day you dug out that old pair of binoculars your dad used in the Navy. And bingo! You became a birdwatcher – or at least you were well on your way.

But if you're going to do it properly, you need to get the right kit. Those ancient binoculars may look impressive, but the lenses are scratched and, besides, they're so heavy you can't be bothered to take them out of the house. And that beautifully illustrated book on birds of the world may be handy if you're in the Amazon rainforest, African savannah or the wilds of Alaska, but it isn't much use at telling Blue and Great Tits apart.

It's time to bite the bullet, raid the bank account and invest in your future hobby.

THE BASIC KIT

Birdwatchers love bits of kit. In fact, given the amount of gear that some people carry it's a wonder they don't do themselves an injury. But you don't actually have to own a telescope the size of a supergun, or a collection of books to rival the British Library, to enjoy watching birds. All you really need, at least to get started, are three items:

1 a pair of binoculars, to get close-up views of birds;
2 a field notebook, to write down what you've seen;
3 a field guide, to help you tell the different species apart.

Simple, isn't it? And they won't cost you a fortune. Of course, you can spend more or less as much as you like on equipment, but these three items can be obtained for under £100 for the lot.

Binoculars

A pair of binoculars is every birdwatcher's most vital and treasured item of equipment. We feel naked without our 'bins', as most birders call them. We need to feel that reassuring weight around our neck, like a security blanket, ready for action if a bird should suddenly fly overhead.

How binoculars work

Binoculars work in a very simple way: they magnify the image you're looking at to make it seem much closer than it actually is. Until you've looked at a bird through a decent pair of bins, you don't know what you're missing. More than anything else, they will transform your interest in birds from a casual pastime into an all-consuming passion.

Types of binoculars

There are three basic types of binoculars:
- **Conventional, or 'porro-prism'.** These are the 'classic'-shaped binoculars, and the type beginners are most likely to start off with. Make sure you buy a pair with coated lenses, which give a better-quality image. They are generally sturdy, if sometimes on the heavy side, and if you buy a good-quality pair, they will last for years.
- **Roof-prism.** These are the top-of-the-range binoculars, costing upwards of £600 a pair. They are more streamlined in shape than porro-prism models, and their ability to gather light at one end and transmit it to your eyes at the other is generally better. Another

BINOCULARS
the technical stuff

Binoculars come in all shapes and sizes – and at prices to match! So how do you tell them apart?

On every pair of binoculars there are two figures that look like a multiplication sum – for example, 8 x 30 or 10 x 50. The first of these figures (e.g. 8x or 10x) refers to the power of magnification. So a pair of 8x bins brings whatever you're looking at eight times closer, while 10x brings it ten times closer, and so on.

But a word of warning – you shouldn't simply go for the most powerful pair with the highest magnification. That's because the higher the figure, the narrower the 'field of view' of the binoculars, and the less bright the image. Also, quality varies enormously with price, and sharpness and light-gathering ability are more important than power.

The second of the two figures (e.g. 30, 40 or 50) is also a factor here. This figure refers to the diameter, in millimetres, of the objective lenses – the big ones at the front. The larger the number, the more light the lenses let in. The more light, the brighter the image, and the wider the field of view.

You can do a simple sum to compare the brightness and field of view of different pairs of binoculars. This involves dividing the first number into the second, to produce a single figure. So, for example, for a pair of 10 x 50s, divide 50 by 10, and you get the figure 5. For 7 x 42s, the figure is 6, for 8 x 30s, it is just under 4, and so on. When comparing binoculars in the same price range, the higher the figure, the better the light transmission of the binoculars, and the wider the field of view.

Buying binoculars always involves a level of compromise: do you do most of your birding in wide open spaces, where the birds are quite far away? If so, you'll want a higher magnification – say 10x. But if you generally watch birds in woodlands, where you need a wide field of view, or at dawn or dusk, when brightness is important, then choose a pair of 7x or 8x, with a wide objective lens (greater than 40mm if possible).

advantage is that they are more compact, and generally lighter in weight, than conventional models.

• **Compact.** There are many compacts on the market, generally aimed at the casual user. Although a few are excellent, unless you pay a high price they tend to suffer from the compromises needed to reduce their size and weight. Compacts have their uses, for example, as a second pair to carry around with you all the time, but are not really recommended as your main pair of binoculars.

Choosing binoculars

So how do you go about choosing your first pair of bins? In roughly descending order of importance, here are our top ten tips:

1 **Don't cut corners** by getting them from a high street shop or mail order company. You may save a few quid, but you'll soon regret it. Go instead to one of the specialist dealers advertised in the monthly birding magazines (see page 216).

2 Buy the best possible binoculars you can afford. A good pair can last for years or even a lifetime, so try to stretch your budget as far as you can – you won't regret it. Consider buying a good second-hand pair, so long as the dealer has serviced them and gives you a guarantee.

3 Size isn't everything. New birders often make the mistake of choosing the pair with the highest magnification. Sounds logical, after all. But odd as it may seem, a pair of 7x or 8x bins is often better than a 10x or 12x. That's because, as explained opposite, the higher the magnification, the duller the image, the narrower the field of view, and the heavier they are to carry.

4 Which brings us on to **brightness.** The lower the magnification, and the wider the objective lens, the brighter the image (again, see opposite). So if you plan to do a lot of your birding at dawn or dusk, choose a pair of 7 x 42 or 8 x 40.

5 A lower magnification and larger objective lens also bring the benefit of a **wider field of view.** This is particularly useful when watching woodland birds, which tend to flit around rapidly from twig to twig.

6 Check close focus. There's nothing more frustrating than watching a bird that has come too close for your binoculars to focus. Most decent bins should focus down to 4 metres (13 ft) or so.

7 Watch your weight. The binoculars may not seem heavy in the shop, but after a long day in the field, every extra ounce feels like a lead weight around your neck. Heavier bins are also harder to keep steady, especially during prolonged use.

8 Go for a 'test-drive'. All reputable retailers will allow you to test a selection of binoculars. Some hold regular open days at bird reserves, others let you nip outside the shop, so long as you leave behind some kind of security. So don't part with your money until you've done a thorough field-test, checking that they are easy to focus and that the image is sharp and clear right to the edge.

9 Buy what feels right for you. Don't just get the ones your friend likes. Binoculars are a very personal thing, so choose the pair that feels comfortable in your hands and gives you the clearest and brightest image.

10 Once you've bought a pair of binoculars, **look after them.** In the right hands, a good pair of bins will last a lifetime. So don't drop them, scratch the lenses, spill food on them, leave them out in the rain, put them on your car roof and drive off, or lend them to anyone – and that means anyone! Do handle them carefully, clean the lenses regularly with a soft brush and lens tissue, and look after them as if they were a new-born baby.

Using binoculars

You've bought your first pair of 'real' binoculars, and you're dying to try them out. But the birds just don't seem to be cooperating. Even when you do manage to get one in view, it looks all fuzzy, or all you can see is a double-image.

Before you rush back to the shop to complain, try some simple tests:

- **Are the eyepieces the right distance apart?** Most people set them too far apart – the best way to get it right is to focus on something fairly close, then push the eyepieces together until the double image becomes a single one.
- **Check the eyepieces.** As well as the central focusing wheel or knob, most bins have a separate focus mechanism on one of the eyepieces, to compensate for any differences between your eyes. Once you've set this, fasten the knob into position with a small piece of tape.
- **Finally, if you wear spectacles,** but your eyesight isn't too bad, take them off while birding. But if this means you can't actually see any birds, make sure you buy a pair of bins with either rubber or push-down eyepieces. Folding them down will give you a far wider field of view.

FIELDCRAFT
watching birds with binoculars

Watching birds with binoculars isn't as easy as it sounds, especially at first. One method is to hold the binoculars just below your eyes as you scan. Once you see a bird, bring the bins up to your eyes rapidly but smoothly. For more distant birds, practise scanning from left to right along a line, stopping when something of interest appears in view.

Focusing can also be difficult, especially at close range. There is no real substitute for practice. Try to get used to the direction of your focus mechanism, and test it out in as many different situations as possible.

Shake can be another problem. Learn to hold your bins so that your arms are comfortable. For long periods of watching, rest on a wall or fence, or against a tree – anything to minimize the amount of shaking.

These teething troubles soon pass, and before long you'll begin to think of your binoculars as an extension of your eyesight, and the fun can really begin.

Field notebook

Next to your binoculars, a field notebook is one of your most essential items of equipment. You can use it to:

* make a list of the different species you see, and how many individual birds are present;
* write down notes of bird behaviour, both commonplace and unusual;
* take notes on any species you can't identify, to help you work out their identity later.

Learning to make detailed, accurate field notes is one of the basic skills of birdwatching. Field notes help you develop your skills at identifying birds and understanding their behaviour and habits. They also provide you with a permanent record of your birding experiences.

USING A DIGITAL RECORDER

As an alternative to pen and paper, you can use a miniature digital recorder to make field notes. These handy little machines allow you to record and store hours of material, which you can either download onto your PC and keep, or simply use to make notes of what you have seen when you get home.

The advantage of this method is that you can speak faster than you can write and, in winter, your fingers don't get frozen. This enables you to capture the essential details of the bird's appearance before it disappears from view.

The downside is that the battery may go flat just as you press the 'record' button, when you're watching the birds of a lifetime. Or you may accidentally erase a whole track of notes. But in general these are pretty foolproof, and a real asset in the field.

More or less any notebook will do, so long as it's sturdy enough to stand up to life in the field, and pages don't fall out every time you open it. Some people prefer loose-leaf notebooks, others a standard one – it's up to you.

Field guide

A field guide is simply a book that tells you what different kinds of bird look like. There is, after all, a limit to the enjoyment you can derive from watching birds without knowing which species they belong to. Once you know whether a bird is a Coot or a Moorhen, a Blue Tit or a Great Tit, a Willow Warbler or a Chiffchaff, you can begin to find the answers to questions like: Where does it live? Where has it come from? Why does it behave in that way (see Chapter 5)?

Which of the many field guides now on the market should you buy? Well, that depends on how and where you're planning to use it. Do you only watch birds in the British Isles, or abroad as well? Do you want something simple, with a single portrait of every common species, or a more complete guide, with pictures of the birds in a variety of different plumages and in flight? Do you want it to fit in your pocket, or will you only use it at home as a work of reference?

The iconic red breast of the Robin – a fairly common but always welcome sight.

There is no perfect field guide for beginners. So take a good look

at several (you will find a list in Further Reading, page 216) and choose one with most, if not all, of the following features:

- **A limited number of species.** At first, you may prefer to stick with guides that cover just the birds of the British Isles, rather than all kinds of exotic European species you're not likely to see here.
- **Ease of use.** The best guides are those with text and illustration on facing pages, or the same page, to avoid having to thumb through the book to find what you're looking for.
- Birds illustrated in a **range of plumages** (see Chapter 2) and **poses.**
- **Not too bulky or heavy.** You should be able to carry it in a jacket or coat pocket for use in the field.

Once you've chosen your guide, take it out and test it against familiar species. Be critical. Field guides are not Holy Writ, and their authors and illustrators are not infallible: mistakes can and do occur.

This may sound a bit like going back to school, but it's also worth spending a bit of time testing yourself. Borrow a selection of guides from the library or a friend, cover up the captions and text and try to identify the pictures. Better still, get a friend to read out the descriptions (remembering to leave out any words that give the bird's identification away!).

Finally, beware the 'it must be a such-and-such' syndrome. Just as every UFO sighting produces a string of copycat reports, so having a picture of a bird before your eyes can lead you to make all kinds of assumptions. Make sure you look at the bird itself, and remember there is no substitute for good views and detailed, accurate field notes.

Clothes for birding

It's easy to identify the wrong kind of clothes for birding – too light and too bright. What's fine for a quick Sunday afternoon stroll won't keep you warm and dry on Blakeney Point in February, or Shetland in summer! And the day-glo outfits favoured by mountaineers will distract other birdwatchers as well as frightening off the birds. So:

- **Wear something comfortable.** You'll be wearing these clothes for long periods of time, in different weather conditions, both sitting and standing – if they rub you in the wrong places, don't buy them.

• **Wear something dull.** Birds have very good colour vision, so bright colours may frighten them off before you get close enough to identify them.

• **Wear something windproof.** Many good sites are on the coast, and exposed to greater wind speeds than in sheltered inland spots.

• **Wear something waterproof.** It always rains! Gore-Tex and similar fabrics are designed to be breathable, taking away moisture from inside while remaining windproof and waterproof on the outside.

• **Wear several layers.** This not only keeps you warmer, but will enable you to remove or add a layer as your body temperature rises or falls. This is especially important if, as often happens while birding, you spend part of the time on the move and part standing still. Many birders have now discarded thick, heavy, traditional jackets in favour of the 'fleece-and-shell' system, in which one or two warm fleeces are worn beneath a lightweight waterproof top.

• **Wear something with large pockets,** for your notebook, field guide, sandwiches, spectacles, chocolate bars and so on.

• **Remember your hands and feet.** Gloves are essential, as even on spring and autumn days the weather can suddenly turn cold. Once again, the layer principle works best, with a thin pair worn under a thicker one to enable you to write field notes and focus your bins. Warm, waterproof boots or shoes are also vital, as you never know when you'll want to walk through mud or wet grass, even in summer.

As with optical equipment and books, there are several specialist clothing suppliers who advertise in the monthly birding magazines (see page 216). Otherwise, try your local camping or outdoor pursuits shop – but remember, avoid shocking pink!

2 WHAT'S THAT BIRD?

IDENTIFYING BIRDS

You've got your binoculars, notebook and field guide, and you're raring to go. But when you get out in the field, you find things aren't quite as straightforward as perhaps you hoped. Some species are easy to identify: a Robin, Blackbird or Magpie, for example. Others clearly

Left The Wren is Britain's commonest bird, with around 10 million breeding pairs.

Right Male and female House Sparrows have distinctive plumages: the male *(left in the picture)* is brighter, with a grey and chestnut head pattern and black bib.

belong to a particular group: ducks, geese or gulls, say – but telling which particular species you're looking at is a bit trickier.

Then there are those birds that don't look like anything you've ever seen before and leave you feeling baffled and frustrated. At these times, it can seem as if all other birders are identification experts, able to tell the identity of any bird at a glance.

But don't despair! Given a little time and experience, you'll soon find that you can identify most of the birds you see.

BEGIN AT THE BEGINNING

More than 550 different species of bird have, at one time or another, been seen in the wild in the British Isles. But before this figure daunts you, we should add that around two-thirds of these are either very rare visitors, or scarce passage migrants, found mainly on remote offshore islands and headlands. A further fifty or so are confined to specialized habitats or localities. So to start with at least you only need to get to grips with around 100 different species.

You might be surprised to learn that the commonest bird in the British Isles is the Wren, with around 10 million breeding pairs. However, because Wrens are shy and unobtrusive birds, you may not see them very often. Other species with several million breeding pairs include the Blackbird, Chaffinch, Robin, House Sparrow and Starling.

In fact, just thirty species account for three-quarters of Britain's 120 million or so birds.

SPOT THE DIFFERENCE

However, there is a catch. Birds don't just come in a single model for each species. Some, like the Mallard, have distinctive male and female plumages. Others, like the Black-headed Gull, have a different dress during the breeding season from the rest of the year. And with many birds, the young look quite different from the adults.

The variety of plumages within the same species can cause headaches for the beginner, as a flock of apparently different-looking birds may turn out to be different plumage types of the same species.

When birds are passing from one plumage state to another (juvenile to adult, or breeding to non-breeding, for example), they often appear quite tatty, which may cause confusion as to their true identity. This is because they are undergoing moult: the replacement of one group of feathers with another.

Here's a quick guide to the different varieties of bird plumage:

Male and female

In quite a few species, the male and female have different plumages – known as sexual dimorphism. Ducks are probably the best known in this respect, but birds-of-prey, the Blackbird, Chaffinch and House Sparrow, are other examples. There are two reasons for this: the male's brighter plumage attracts females, and the female's duller plumage enables her to conceal herself from predators when sitting on the nest.

Because they stay the same for all or most of the year, these are probably the easiest plumages to learn. But beware of the strange plumage worn by ducks in mid-summer, known as 'eclipse'. During moult, the bright males become dark and dingy and often look very peculiar indeed, causing problems for the unwary beginner.

Breeding and non-breeding

Look in any field guide and chances are that it will refer to the seasonal plumage changes of species like the Great Crested Grebe as 'summer' and 'winter' plumages. This can be misleading, especially when you see grebes in full 'summer' plumage in the middle of winter. That's why most birders now refer to these as 'breeding' and 'non-breeding' plumages.

Birds don't follow quite the same calendar as we do: if the weather is mild, their 'spring' may start as early as January, so look out for birds moulting into breeding plumage soon after the New Year.

The second moult, into the drabber non-breeding plumage, may start as soon as the young birds have fledged (that is, left the nest and flown): as early as mid-summer for some species. But late breeders may hang on to their breeding finery until well into the autumn.

Juvenile, immature and adult

No bird has the same plumage throughout the whole of its life. Birds are born either without feathers or with a downy covering. When they fledge they are covered with their first true feathers, known as 'juvenile' plumage.

Songbirds, like the Robin and House Sparrow, go straight from juvenile to adult plumage, by moulting their feathers in the autumn after hatching.

Other, longer-lived birds like gulls go through several different plumages before they reach adulthood.

Gull plumages can be so difficult to distinguish that even experienced birders fall back on the catch-all term 'immature' – which really just means the bird is no longer a chick, but isn't yet in full adult plumage!

Midsummer to early autumn is the time to watch out for unusual plumages, which often turn out to be on young birds. Many a new birder has been puzzled by the appearance of the juvenile Robin, which is a rather dull, spotty brown, lacking the adult's red breast. If you're unsure of a young bird's identity, try to concentrate on its size, shape and behaviour, which normally give its identity away.

Also in autumn, beware the variety of plumages in groups like waders, where the juveniles appear clean and fresh, as their feathers are new, while the adults sport a dull, worn plumage, making them appear quite different from the young birds.

Above A pair of Great Crested Grebes in full breeding plumage.
Left Three ages of Herring Gulls: full adult on the left, juvenile in the centre and a second-summer on the right.

IDENTIFYING BIRDS IN FLIGHT

Many a birder has prayed for a field guide that portrays every species from behind, so that they can identify the bird as it flies rapidly away from them! In fact, birds can be identified in flight, so long as you know what to look for.

Flying birds often look quite different from the way you'd expect. A flying Moorhen, for example, appears very unfamiliar until it lands and adopts its characteristic jerky pose. Ducks and waders in flight often show unexpected flashes of colour or white, which can be confusing or helpful.

A Harrier flying overhead panics a Moorhen but causes a Green Sandpiper to reveal its characteristic white rump.

Then there's the problem of the angle of view. Many birds, especially birds-of-prey and gulls, are often seen from below, as they soar high into the clouds above your head. Here, wing-shape and pattern are very important, with quite small differences distinguishing one species from another. Even then, you won't manage to identify them all, and there will always be 'the one that got away'.

So, once again, the best way to learn is to get out there and have a go. And don't forget your notebook!

MAKING FIELD NOTES

The golden rule in making field notes is to get down the essential points straightaway. Don't waste time noting down details of the habitat, weather conditions, or date and time of the sighting – all these can wait until after the bird has flown off. Instead, concentrate on the essentials:

- **Size and shape.** Preferably by comparing the bird with other species present at the same time – is it larger or smaller? Brighter or duller? Does it have more or less white on the wing? Also note down details of the bird's shape and posture – is it fat or thin? Horizontal or vertical?
- **Plumage details.** Start at the head and work methodically through the different parts of the body, not forgetting the 'bare parts' (the bill, legs and feet). Concentrate on things which stand out, known as 'diagnostic' features.
- **Behaviour.** Was the bird hopping or walking? Swimming or diving?
- **Song or call** (if appropriate).

When you've got everything you need on the bird itself, turn to the **extra details.** Make a note of the date and time, direction and quality of light, and the weather conditions.

Don't forget details of the bird's **habitat** and **behaviour.** These can be invaluable when you come to the process of elimination by which you try to put an identity to the bird. So a small brown bird flying high in the sky above arable farmland and singing its heart out is more likely to be a Skylark than a Nightingale. Conversely, if it's deep inside a thicket in a deciduous woodland in spring, it's probably not a Skylark – unless it's well and truly lost!

You'll soon learn what you should and shouldn't include. At first, it's best to err on the side of too much detail rather than too little, even if you seem to be spending more time scribbling notes about the birds than actually watching them!

It's always tempting to write down something you *think* you saw, or expected to see. Don't. If you didn't see the bird's leg colour, say so. And whatever you do, don't try to 'fill in the gaps' by referring to field guides.

Finally, always keep your field notebooks safe. You'll be surprised how enjoyable it is to pick them up a few years later, and re-read your accounts of memorable days in the field.

FIELD SKETCH

If you can, do a quick sketch of the bird in your notebook. However bad your drawing skills, it will at least help you to pinpoint the key field marks (see also Drawing and painting birds, page 95).

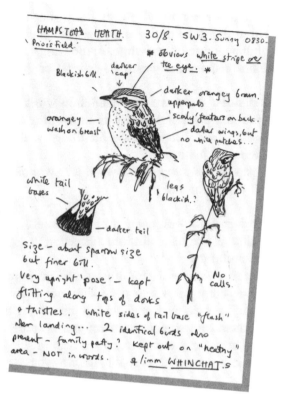

HAMPSTEAD HEATH. 30/8. SW3. Sunny 0830.
'Prior's Field.'

※ obvious white stripe over the eye. ※

Blackish G.M. darker 'cap'

darker orangey brown. upperparts
'scaly' feathers on back.
darker wings, but no white patches...

orangey wash on breast

white tail bases

legs blackish.?

darker tail

Size - about sparrow size but finer G.M.
Very upright 'pose' - kept flitting along tops of docks & thistles. White sides of tail base "flash" when landing... 2 identical birds also present - family party? kept out on "heathy" area - NOT in woods.
⚥ /imm WHINCHAT.s

No calls.

BIRD TOPOGRAPHY

Bird topography refers to the external features and feather-patterns of a bird – it's a kind of map of the bird's body. Each part of the bird is given a particular name, so that two birdwatchers looking at two different birds in different places can produce accurate, unambiguous descriptions.

At first, using terms like 'primaries' instead of wing-feathers, or supercilium instead of eyebrow, can seem a bit complicated and unnecessary. But with some more difficult-to-identify species, a cast-iron identity can only be established if you do. So it's a good idea to get into the habit right from the start.

SIZE DIFFERENCES AND LIGHT CONDITIONS

Look in any field guide, and you'll find the first thing mentioned about any bird is its size. So we learn that a Blackbird is 25 cm (10 in) long, a

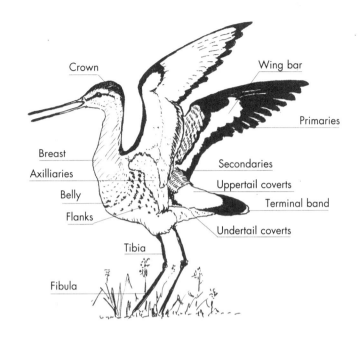

Crown

Wing bar

Primaries

Breast

Axilliaries

Belly

Flanks

Secondaries

Uppertail coverts

Terminal band

Undertail coverts

Tibia

Fibula

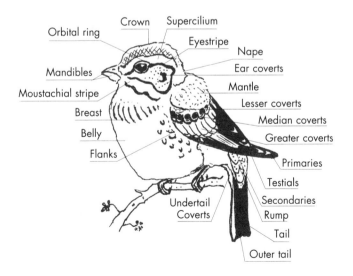

Orbital ring

Crown   Supercilium

Eyestripe

Nape

Mandibles

Ear coverts

Moustachial stripe

Mantle

Breast

Lesser coverts

Belly

Median coverts

Flanks

Greater coverts

Primaries

Testials

Undertail
Coverts

Secondaries

Rump

Tail

Outer tail

Goldcrest (Britain's smallest bird) only 9 cm (3.5 in) and a Mute Swan (our largest) up to 160 cm (63 in).

But what does this actually mean to a birder in the field? Not very much, really. For example, a Dunlin is about the same length as a Skylark, but because it's a bulkier bird and a different shape it looks a lot bigger. Also, size can be misleading. Birds fluff up their plumage in the cold, or hold themselves in an unusual posture, and this affects our perception of their size.

Think about it. If someone held up a book, or a children's toy, anything between 50 and 200 metres (60 and 120 yards) away from you, would you be confident of assessing its size to the nearest centimetre or so? Yet that's just what many birders do when they confidently proclaim that the wader they're watching is 'about Dunlin-sized'.

What they really mean is that it reminds them of a Dunlin, therefore it must be Dunlin-sized. A catalogue of mistaken identifications suggests that birders are in fact very bad at judging size, especially that of a lone bird, when there are no others for comparison.

Distance is another problem. A bird can appear very different depending on how far away it really is, especially through high-powered optical aids. So don't jump to conclusions. As the old joke goes, 'Is it a bird? Is it a plane?' Is it a fly on the end of my telescope?'

Finally, remember that light conditions can change dramatically, depending on the time of day, time of year and state of the weather. The same bird can appear quite differently coloured, depending, for example, on whether it is backlit, or observed at dawn, or in the bright midday sun.

ESCAPES AND EXOTICS

Every now and then, you come across a bird you simply can't identify. You've taken notes, checked the field guides and racked your brains, yet it's still a mystery. When this happens the chances are it's an 'escape' – a former cage or aviary bird which has managed to break free, and is now wandering at large.

Escapes come in all shapes and sizes. It has been said that almost every one of the world's 9000 or so species of bird, apart perhaps from swifts, could be kept in captivity – and many of them are. The most popular are waterfowl, finches and buntings, and brightly coloured tropical birds like parrots. However, many other species are kept as cagebirds, and escape from time to time. Undesirable as keeping birds in captivity may seem, a spacious and well-maintained aviary does offer an opportunity of watching exotic birds to people who might otherwise never get the opportunity.

In day-to-day birdwatching, you're most likely to encounter exotic ducks, budgies, or common seed-eaters such as zebra finches and waxbills. Nowadays, local bird recorders are beginning to record these systematically, as in the past escaped species like the Ruddy Duck and Ring-necked Parakeet have established self-sufficient feral populations. Today's escape may be tomorrow's 'official' British bird, so if you come across one, don't ignore it!

LEARNING BIRD SONGS AND CALLS

When it comes to bird identification, new birdwatchers tend to concentrate on the appearance of a bird. This is all fine and dandy until you come across those species that either look very similar, or spend their time hidden from view in trees or bushes, like the Willow Warbler and Chiffchaff. This is where a thorough knowledge of bird song comes into its own.

The difference between bird song and bird calls is not always straightforward. Normally, however, the song is a complex series of notes, sung by the male, and designed to do two things: defend a territory and attract a mate.

Bird calls, on the other hand, can be made by males or females, adults or young. They generally consist of a single note, or simple series of notes, and have a specific purpose: for example, to sound an alarm, make contact with others in a flock, or beg a parent for food. You'll find more about bird calls and song in Chapter 5, and in Bill's entry for the end of September in his year-round account of birding on Hampstead Heath (see page 145).

Identifying birds by song

Many birders find identifying birds by song alone difficult. There are, however, a number of ways in which you can ease the pain of learning. The first is to use mnemonics: little reminders that help you remember a particular species' call or song.

FIELDCRAFT – JIZZ

Jizz is the secret weapon in the birder's armoury, using your capacity for memory and intuition to the full. After all, we are meant to be smarter than the birds, aren't we?

You've come across an unfamiliar bird. Chances are that in the next few seconds it will fly away, never to be seen again. DON'T PANIC! Try to stay calm and think clearly. Does it look like a bird you've seen before? Roughly what category of birds does it come into – is it 'duck-like', 'sparrow-like', and so on? Is it about thrush-sized? Pigeon-sized? Wandering albatross-sized?

Even without knowing it, you're already taking advantage of a vital concept known as 'jizz'. The word jizz has a mysterious pedigree, but may partly derive from US Air Force slang for 'general impression and shape', or 'gis'. Wherever the word comes from, jizz simply refers to the 'feel' of a bird. It enables an experienced birder to know what species they're looking at, even if the bird is too far away to see any plumage details.

Think of the way you can pick out a familiar face from a crowd because of some indefinable combination of features. A short, bearded birder in a green anorak is Bill, for example.

Well, birds are the same. So a sleek, long-winged bird hovering above a roadside is almost certainly a Kestrel. A huge, broad-winged, long-legged bird near water is a Grey Heron. You'll soon get the hang of it.

Jizz will never be a substitute for detailed notes on plumage, but it can point you in the right direction, by narrowing down the choice of potential species. But beware: just because a bird looks like a duck, swims like a duck and is found alongside ducks, it may not actually be a duck. It could be a Coot or Moorhen: birds of the rail family which have evolved to look like ducks!

A Hobby flying overhead can be identified by its distinctive jizz: slender body, swept-back wings and fast flight.

For example, the Great Tit's song repeats two notes, and sounds a bit as though the bird is saying 'tea-cher, tea-cher, tea-cher', with the stress on the second syllable. The Willow Warbler's accelerates in a rapid run from high to low notes – rather like a pianist doing a run down the scale.

As you listen to a bird singing, try to devise your own memory aids to remember its song. These can be highly imaginative – as in one birder's comparison of the Chaffinch's song to a fast bowler delivering a ball! Try it out next time you hear a Chaffinch.

The main aspects of bird song to concentrate on are tone, pitch and rhythm. Try to think of each bird as a jazz musician, weaving an improvised melody from the basic kit of notes. Most birds have a characteristic way of singing that gives away their identity.

So if you hear a song coming from deep in a reedbed in spring, listen for the rhythm. If it is a series of harsh, repeated notes in sets of two or three, it's almost certainly a Reed Warbler. If, on the other hand, it is far less structured, with occasional whistles and trills, it is probably a Sedge Warbler. Even so, try to catch a glimpse of the bird to verify your identification.

Bird calls

Calls are much more problematic – especially as most birds seem to make a monosyllabic tweeting sound! But with practice and experience you'll soon begin to distinguish between species you see and hear regularly.

Tone is very important in distinguishing one bird call from another. Some calls sound deep and fluty; others are high and thin. But remember that a single species can demonstrate a bewildering repertoire of calls, so don't jump to conclusions.

Some birders use an artificial 'bird call' to attract birds. This is a small metal object rather like a child's whistle, which you twist and turn, producing a squeaking noise.

Another technique much practised in North America, and becoming increasingly popular on this side of the Atlantic, is pishing. This is designed to help you get a good sighting of an elusive bird, especially in autumn and winter. It works like this. You purse your lips and place them against the back of your hand. Then, you begin to make 'kissing' noises. With luck, the bird's curiosity is aroused, and it emerges from the bush in front of you and performs in front of your eyes.

SOUND ON THE MOVE

Another good way to learn bird songs and calls is to take advantage of the latest new technology. We used to take tapes or CDs into the field, but these are awkward and bulky. Nowadays, digital technology means you can store as many bird sounds and calls as you want onto your portable MP3 player or smartphone, either through commercially available Apps or by downloading from CDs.

But you won't really get to grips with bird song until you've tried out your knowledge for real, in the field. It's best to go in early spring, when the courtship ritual is in full swing and male birds are singing to defend a territory and win a mate. Start with the common, familiar birds then broaden your knowledge by visiting new habitats with a wider variety of species.

From a practical point of view, it's also a lot easier to catch sight of singing birds in February or March, before the trees come into leaf. It helps your confidence no end if you can clinch the identification by actually seeing the bird as it sings.

Later in the spring, when summer visitors begin to return, you can extend your knowledge by listening to the various new arrivals, such as the warblers. By the end of the breeding season, when everything has gone quiet, you should be more confident at identifying birds by sound alone. Just make sure you keep practising during the autumn and winter, or by the following spring you may have forgotten it all again!

One theory is that pishing sounds like the contact calls made by small birds to attract other members of their flock to food, or perhaps warning of danger, so they come to see what all the fuss is about. Either that, or they just want to have a good laugh at you making a fool of yourself.

In fact, pishing does seem to work. But if you're too embarrassed to try the traditional method, you may prefer to adopt a more refined approach. You don't have to kiss your hand – instead just make a repeated 'pish-pish-pish' noise.

A word of warning, however. One birdwatcher did such a good impression of a flock of tits that a Sparrowhawk crashed through the bushes and hit him right in the face. Fortunately, he had just raised his binoculars to his eyes, so he wasn't hurt – just very shocked!

Right The Sedge Warbler's song is full of unexpected sounds and notes, quite different from the rhythmic song of the Reed Warbler.

Left The Yellowhammer's song is often rendered in words, 'a-little-bit-of-bread-and-no-cheeeeese'.

3 BIRDING BEGINS AT HOME

One of the best places to begin watching birds is at home – especially if you have a garden. They're great places for birds, for many reasons.

First, the trees and bushes provide a safe place to shelter, roost, build nests and raise young. Second, gardens are often a lot more productive, food-wise, than the surrounding urban jungle or factory-farmed fields. Finally, gardens are the best place for birds to get a free lunch – and indeed breakfast, dinner and tea – thanks to the food we supply for them.

But providing food doesn't just benefit the birds – it also gives us the chance to enjoy close-up views of a wide variety of common and not-so-common species. Because they are usually at close range, and tend to stick around to feed, birds in gardens also provide an ideal opportunity to learn more about bird identification and behaviour. And, of course, the opportunity of watching birds in the garden from the comfort of indoors is ideal for anyone who is housebound.

ATTRACTING BIRDS TO YOUR GARDEN

Feeding garden birds used to be so simple: you just threw a few scraps of stale bread on to the lawn and waited for the birds to arrive. But now there's a whole range of hi-tech equipment and foodstuffs available, guaranteed to please even the most discerning diner. It's well worth considering these in detail to make your garden a favourite port of call with the birds.

Bird tables

The centrepiece of a bird 'feeding-station' (see page 41) is the bird table. Beware the ornamental varieties found in garden centres, which may look attractive but aren't usually very good at their job, because they do not normally offer the birds and their food protective cover.

The main purpose of a bird table is to provide a sturdy platform for the birds to feed, and shelter, in the form of a roof, to stop the food getting wet and spoiling. An added feature is that you can hang peanut and seed feeders from the base of the table itself.

If you have a talent for carpentry, you can build your own bird table, but most people prefer to buy one. Go to a reputable supplier, such as the RSPB (see page 214), and you shouldn't have to pay more than £20 or so for a table that will last for years.

Food dispensers

The bird table itself is just the start. For years Americans have used all manner of ingenious food dispensers to attract birds into gardens; now these are available on this side of the Atlantic too.

- **Peanut feeders,** made from sturdy wire-mesh and hung from a washing line or tree, are widely available and cheap, costing around £5 each. These will soon become a regular rendezvous for the local tit population, though House Sparrows and Starlings often monopolize them at the expense of smaller birds.
- **Seed feeders** are even better – especially when filled with nutritious and tasty sunflower seeds. These have small perches for the birds to land on, and holes to dispense the seeds gradually, preventing wastage and mess. Like the peanut feeders, they are light enough to hang from a branch or bird table. Costing anything between £7 and £30, depending on size, seed feeders are especially popular with Blue and Great Tits, Greenfinches and Siskins.
- **Squirrel-proof feeders.** It can be very frustrating to put out food for tits and finches, only to see it taken by larger birds like Starlings, or stolen by an enterprising squirrel. So some manufacturers have designed feeders especially for smaller birds, with bars to keep out unwelcome visitors. These are more expensive, usually retailing at above the £20 mark, but are well worth considering, especially if you have a problem with Grey Squirrels in your area.
- **Feeding-stations.** At the luxury end of the bird-feeding market, feeding-stations can look like something out of a sci-fi film, and may cause the neighbours to raise a few eyebrows. They can cost anything up to £100, but they are built to last and will provide a valuable service for hungry birds.

Food for birds

Some birds, like Starlings, seem to eat almost anything provided, from kitchen scraps to peanuts. But others have more specialized diets, so if you want to maximize the range of species in your garden, it's worth considering a range of foods.

- **Sunflower seeds** are one step up from peanuts, and though they are a little more expensive they provide excellent nutritional value all year round.
- **Smaller seeds,** such as wheat or corn, are ideal to put on a bird table, or to give ground feeders such as sparrows and pigeons. Don't put too much food out at once, though, or you may attract unwelcome visitors such as rats.
- **Food bars,** containing a rich mixture of oily foods, provide valuable energy for smaller birds during periods of cold winter weather.
- **Live food,** such as mealworms, is especially popular with Robins, Dunnocks, Blackbirds and thrushes.

Incidentally, if you do continue to feed peanuts to birds, make sure you obtain them from a reputable supplier, as there have been several cases of cheap peanuts poisoning birds that fed on them.

When should you feed garden birds?

Most people feed birds in their garden throughout the winter months, which is when they need food the most. In cold weather, songbirds need to eat the equivalent of around one-quarter of their body weight each day simply to survive, so the food provided in gardens is a vital lifeline.

Until recently, experts advised people to stop feeding birds in the spring, as there were reports of baby tits choking on peanuts brought by the adult birds. However, the BTO now advise us to continue feeding through the spring and summer months, as the adult birds need all the nutrition they can get.

On the other hand the RSPB advise that in spring and summer it is best to avoid peanuts, and switch to seeds or live foods, as these are the best substitute for the birds' natural insect food. Don't forget that if you've established a feeding programme, the birds will come to rely on you. So, if you're going to be away, arrange for someone to check that the bird table is well stocked in your absence.

A variety of different feeders will attract a wide range of birds, including sparrows, tits and finches.

Bird baths

Food isn't the only lifeline for garden birds. Water, too, is essential, especially in cold winter weather when other sources are likely to be frozen over. You can buy a ready-made bird bath, or make your own out of a shallow dish, but whatever you do, make sure that the water is clean and regularly changed, and that you break the ice when temperatures drop below freezing!

Also, make sure that the water isn't more than a few centimetres deep, and that the bath's sides are shallow, to make it easier for the birds to drink and bathe. See also Garden ponds (page 46).

Beware of the cat (and other hazards)!

Gardens may be a welcome larder for wild birds, but they are also one of the most dangerous places to visit. Cats are the biggest problem, killing tens of millions of birds every year, often while the birds are busy feeding. However, there are a few things you can do to reduce the death toll:

• Position your feeders in a safe place, away from cover where a cat could hide to stalk its prey.
• Reduce the amount of cover around the feeder by cutting back twigs and branches where a cat might perch.
• If you own a cat yourself, put a loud bell round its neck, and hope the birds hear it coming!

It's also best to avoid putting feeders too near large windows, as birds may not see the glass before it is too late, and get killed in the collision. Alternatively, you can stick a silhouette of a hawk up on the window-pane, which is supposed to frighten the birds off.

Other garden predators include Jays and Magpies and of course the Sparrowhawk. The former two, members of the crow family, generally prey on eggs and chicks rather than adult birds, but the Sparrowhawk will take Blue and Great Tits from right under your nose. Unlike cats, however, at least this magnificent bird of prey is a natural predator.

NESTBOXES AND GARDEN BIRDS

If you want to encourage birds to stay and breed in your garden, there's no better way than by introducing a nestbox. Nestboxes, as their name

NESTBOXES:
hints and tips

• Always buy nestboxes from a reputable supplier, such as the RSPB (see page 214).
• If you do decide to build your own, follow approved plans, also available from the RSPB.
• Put your nestbox up in late winter to give the birds a chance to get used to it.
• Site your nestbox carefully: on a tree, wall or garden fence, 2–5 metres (6–16 ft) above the ground. Also try to face the box in an easterly direction, to avoid the strongest sun and wettest winds. And make sure the box is out of reach of predators and inquisitive children!
• Keep a close eye on your nestbox, especially during the spring, to watch out for prospective tenants. Once you think the birds have taken up residence, never remove the cover or look inside the box, as this may reveal the site to predators, or cause the parents to desert the nest.
• Each autumn, after the young have fledged, check your nestbox and clear out any nesting debris, so that the box is clean and dry for the following year's use.

suggests, are simply artificial substitutes for natural nest-sites, such as holes and cavities in trees.

The best-known nestbox, designed for use by tits, consists of a rectangular-shaped container, made of treated wood or other waterproof material, with a small entrance-hole in the front for the parent birds to enter and leave.

Specialized nestboxes

You can buy or build a nestbox for almost any garden species, from the tiny Wren to large birds like the Kestrel and even Tawny Owl. However, to succeed with species like these generally requires specialist knowledge and experience, so it's best to start off with the standard box and branch out later on.

GARDENING FOR BIRDS

Whether or not you're a keen gardener, there are all sorts of ways to make your garden more attractive to birds. The main thing to remember is that by providing the widest diversity of habitats you will attract the greatest variety of birds. Different species of bird prefer different things: not just food and nesting sites, but also places to roost at night.

Planting for garden birds

The kinds of tree and shrub you plant in your garden will make a huge difference to the birdlife there.

• Try to favour **native species,** such as the hawthorn, or those that provide plenty of berries or fruit, like the varieties of wild cherry.

Left The Waxwing is a rare winter visitor to gardens in eastern Britain. *Below* The Goldfinch has a long, sharp bill for feeding on thistles and teasels.

• Some **non-native plants,** like the various evergreen cypresses, can also provide valuable shelter, and are particularly attractive to Greenfinches. However, they should be planted sparingly, as

they can easily dominate the garden, and overshadow other, more valuable plant habitats.

• **Seed-bearing plants** such as teasels are also highly attractive to finches (especially Goldfinches), and flowers like honeysuckle will attract birds like the Blackcap, which enjoy feeding on nectar.

• Most flowering plants attract **insects,** which will themselves encourage insectivorous birds to visit your garden.

• Allowing at least part of your garden to 'go wild' is also a good way to increase the number and variety of birds there. Try planting a stand of nettles, or a couple of bramble bushes down the back, out of sight. If you want to go further, there are several excellent books on the subject (see Further Reading, page 216). With luck, you should manage to create a habitat that attracts birds without giving the neighbours cause for complaint!

• Remember that birds need the support of plants **throughout the year:** in spring and summer as a place to build nests, in autumn to stock up on nutritious food for the coming cold weather, and in winter as a place to roost and keep warm. So try to design a garden that will provide something for the birds during all four seasons.

Garden ponds

If you really want to broaden the range of species attracted to your garden, one of the best ways to do so is by building a garden pond. Even a small pond can be home to all kinds of insect life and other juicy morsels, and it also provides a valuable place for birds to drink and bathe, and a regular observation point.

A pond can be surprisingly easy to make and not too expensive, although homeowners whose precious goldfish have been stolen by a visiting Heron might not agree! Various books and leaflets containing instructions on how to 'do it yourself' are available, and you can also buy ready-made 'shells'. Make sure that your pond is well stocked with aquatic plants, and keep it clear from fallen leaves, especially in the autumn and winter months.

4 MOVING ON

It won't take long before you begin to look beyond the confines of your garden fence and get the urge to explore new habitats and places. If you want to develop your birdwatching skills and learn more about the way birds live, the best thing to do is to get yourself a 'local patch' (see Bill's year-round account of a very special local patch – Hampstead Heath in north London – on pages 102–155).

A LOCAL PATCH

A local patch is somewhere near your home that you can visit on a regular basis, getting to know the birds that live there. A patch can be anywhere: a local park, small woodland, lake, gravel-pit or reservoir, estuary or even a mountain-top – providing you live close by!

The key to finding a good local patch is access. It should be within easy reach of your home and of a manageable size, so that you can 'cover' it thoroughly in an hour or so, perhaps on the way to or from work, or before breakfast.

Regular visits to your patch will help you create a detailed picture of the resident and visiting birdlife. As the seasons change, you'll notice the comings and goings, and begin to feel that these are 'your' birds – something that brings a real sense of satisfaction.

There are practical benefits in having a patch, too. You'll soon find that you build up quite a knowledge of the local birds: not just of how to identify them, but of their behaviour and habits. And if something

Overleaf Brent Reservoir – looking very exotic at sunset. It's actually next to London's North Circular (Wembley Stadium is in the background) and is very good for birds; an ideal 'local patch'.

HOW TO CHOOSE A LOCAL PATCH

• Explore the local area, within a mile or so of your home. Look for a self-contained 'island' habitat, which will act as a magnet to passing birds, such as a disused gravel pit.
• Make a couple of visits at different times of the day, and note down what you see: not just the different species, but numbers of birds too.
• Once you've chosen your patch, get into the habit of visiting regularly – at least once a week, and more frequently if you can.

unusual drops by, you're more likely to notice it if you're familiar with the usual species.

But 'patchwork' isn't just for your own enjoyment – the birds can benefit as well. If your patch is threatened with development, your records could be a vital weapon in safeguarding its future. So make sure you get into the habit of keeping detailed notes of the birds you see there. Together, Britain's local patches provide an essential lifeline for our birds.

EXPLORING FARTHER AFIELD

Chances are that your patch will contain a range of different habitats: perhaps some trees or bushes, a pond or lake, and more open grassland. (Hampstead Heath – see Bill's chapter on patchwork, pages 102–155 – contains all these in some form – not bad for London!) You'll soon discover that different species tend to favour particular places, something that should help you locate and identify them more easily.

Once you're confident that you can identify the birds on your patch, it's time to explore farther afield, getting to know a wider variety of different families of birds. Before you start, there are a few things you need to bear in mind:

• **Time of day.** Visit a mixed woodland in the middle of the day and it can seem almost devoid of birds, as they are either busy feeding or at rest. But go early in the morning, especially in spring, and the place will be alive with song and activity.

• **Time and tide.** At high tide, wading birds like Dunlin, Redshank and Oystercatcher gather together in huge and spectacular roosts, often giving close views. Then, as the water level begins to drop, they disperse to feed on the vast mudflats of estuaries and coastal marshes. So try to time your visit to coincide with the approaching high tide (see Estuary and coastal marsh, page 58).

• **Time of year.** Birds often change their habitat depending on the time of year. So in winter, woodland breeders like Chaffinches join together with other finches and buntings to feed on stubble-fields. And in spring or autumn, migrants can turn up in all kinds of odd places. So make sure you are aware of the birds likely to be found in a particular habitat at different seasons.

FINDING GOOD SITES

When you begin to explore farther afield, one of your first problems is deciding where to go, and what time of year is best at a particular site. Fortunately there are all sorts of excellent guides to help you, including:

• **'Where to Watch' books.** Since John Gooders' original *Where to Watch Birds* was published in the late 1960s, guides to good bird-watching sites have multiplied. Now you can find out where to go anywhere in the country by using one of the many regional 'where to watch' guides, available in most good bookshops.

• **RSPB Nature Reserves – Information for Visitors.** This is packed with useful information on the society's hundred or so reserves, with times and days of opening, birds you're likely to see, etc. It is available free from the RSPB (see page 214).

• **Seasonal 'itineraries'** in the monthly birding magazines (see page 216). These usually cover a day's birding in a particular area, such as the north Norfolk coast in autumn, or south Devon in spring. They are packed with detailed local knowledge, maps and practical advice.

Bird reserves

Sooner or later you are bound to visit a bird reserve. Bird reserves are not, as some people imagine, full of birds in cages and aviaries – the birds you will see are wild ones! Neither are they pristine areas of 'natural' countryside.

Britain's landscape contains virtually no truly natural habitats, so even bird reserves have been heavily influenced by past forms of land use. This influence continues today, with almost all reserves being intensively managed to create the best possible habitats, to attract a variety of birds.

For example, the RSPB's showpiece reserve at Minsmere, in Suffolk, contains a wide range of habitats from mixed woodland to reedbed and heathland to freshwater marsh. These are subject to constant control, with reeds cut, heathland burned and woods coppiced. If left to themselves, reedbeds would soon turn into birch scrub, and heathlands into woods, endangering rare species like the Bittern and Nightjar, which depend on these artificially maintained habitats for their continued survival.

Hides

There can't be many bird reserves which don't contain at least one hide. These are not the portable canvas ones favoured by bird photographers, but permanent wooden structures, usually placed in a strategic position to enable the occupants to sit and watch birds. Most experienced birders agree that hides have advantages and disadvantages.

The best thing about a hide is that it allows you to get closer than usual to the birds, while sitting in reasonable comfort, sheltered from the wind and rain. You can also share information with the hide's other occupants, making a hide an ideal place for a beginner to sit for an hour or two.

If you do use a hide, don't be afraid to talk to other birdwatchers. Many people think that you must be absolutely silent for fear of frightening away the birds. Nonsense! Birds can easily tolerate the sound of normal human conversation – and if you don't talk to your fellow birders, how will you know what is on view?

However, all hides should also come with a list of 'health warnings'. For a start, even on a sunny day, hides can be extremely cold. By going into a little box you may be restricting your view and missing anything flying overhead or behind the hide. Hides are a difficult place to use a telescope and tripod combination – most birders leave their tripods at the door and attempt to balance the scope by hand. Finally, there are the other occupants. It only takes one loud-mouthed, ignorant person to spoil a hide experience for everybody.

So by all means use hides – but remember, birds can be seen from other places too and often you'll get a better view!

DIFFERENT BIRDS IN DIFFERENT HABITATS

The British Isles is made up of a wide variety of different habitats, from the busy urban skyline to the Caledonian Pine forests of the Scottish Highlands. A whole book could be written about these (indeed several have been!), so this is just a brief guide to the main habitats and the birds found there at different times of year:

Parks and gardens in towns

It's easy to overlook a rich and productive habitat just because it is also one of the most familiar. Many of our common species breed success-fully in parks and gardens, and even more find food there in winter.

Parks can be one of the best places to catch up with species like Green, Great Spotted and Lesser Spotted Woodpeckers, Bullfinch, and Long-tailed Tit, as well as giving close-up views of ducks, geese and swans. Built-up parts of cities and towns support fewer species, although Kestrel and Sparrowhawk may be as easy to see here as anywhere else.
Time of year: With parks, almost any time of year can be productive, although you should forget sunny days in summer, when the birds just hide from the hordes! Spring and autumn mornings can produce a trickle of migrants, while winter may bring sightings of seasonal visitors like the Redwing. The most important thing is to time your visit early enough in the day to avoid dog-walkers.

Farmland

This, more than any other habitat, is one where quality really counts. Sterile prairies whose hedges and hay-meadows have been replaced by mile after mile of wheat or barley can be virtually birdless. But a well-managed, mixed farm with a good variety of habitats can be very productive.

A number of farmland birds, such as Skylark, Grey Partridge, Corn Bunting, Yellowhammer, Tree Sparrow and Lapwing, are in serious decline, mainly because of the changes in land-use over the past few decades. However, with careful searching of the right habitat you should be able to find most of the specialities.

Time of year: After breeding, many species from woodland and wetland habitats gather on farmland to find food for the winter. Look for mixed flocks of finches, buntings and sparrows. Winter thrushes like Redwing and Fieldfare are also highly dependent on farmland.

Mixed or deciduous woodland

This is one of the most productive habitats of all, providing homes for a wide range of breeding and wintering birds, especially tits, warblers, thrushes, woodpeckers and predators such as owls and Sparrowhawk. Specialist feeders like Tree Creeper and Nuthatch are also found here.

Time of year: Early spring sees the start of breeding activity, with the formation of territories, courtship and nest-building. An early-morning visit in April or May should yield a good variety of resident birds and summer visitors. Remember that the earlier in the season, the easier the birds are to see because there are fewer leaves to get in the way!

Late summer and early autumn are usually rather quiet, as songbirds are in moult and tend to hide away. In autumn and winter flocks form, as insect-eating birds like tits and the tiny Goldcrest gather together in search of food to keep alive.

Coniferous woodland

For a long time the vast coniferous forests blanketing Britain's hillsides were regarded as virtually devoid of birdlife. However, more sympathetic management, including the rotation of planting to provide a variety of 'mini-habitats', has brought a greater variety of species. These include the endangered Woodlark and Nightjar, as well as the abundant Coal Tit and Goldcrest, and the rapidly spreading Siskin. A newcomer, the mysterious and elusive Goshawk, is also found in the heart of the forests.

In what remains of the Caledonian Pine Forests of the Scottish Highlands, you can find local specialities such as Crested Tit, Capercaillie and Britain's only endemic species, the Scottish Crossbill.

Time of year: This is a difficult habitat to explore, often being dark and inaccessible. As always, early spring sees the height of breeding activity.

Lowland heath

This is one of Britain's most specialized habitats, with the low density of breeding species more than offset by the rarity of the birds it supports. Most lowland heath is found in southern and eastern England, especially in Dorset, Hampshire, Surrey and East Anglia.

The classic heathland bird is the Dartford Warbler, which is enjoying a population explosion, thanks to the current run of mild winters. Other characteristic heathland species include the Hobby, the Stonechat, the Nightjar and the Woodlark. Most lowland heaths nowadays are protected as nature reserves.

Time of year: Spring is the best season, with breeding activity at its height. But it is worth making another trip in winter which can bring unusual species such as Great Grey Shrike.

Mountains and moorlands

Britain's uplands can provide some of the most rewarding birdwatching experiences of all, though you often have to work hard for your birds. The Scottish mountain-tops play host to some of our rarest breeding species, such as the Golden Eagle, Dotterel and Ptarmigan. Farther north still, the bogs of Sutherland are home to rare breeding waders, like the Greenshank. Moorland is also the stronghold of Red and Black Grouse, and other specialities include Ring Ousel, Hen Harrier, Short-eared Owl and Merlin.

Time of year: A spring or early summer visit is vital if you want to see a reasonable variety of birds, as during the winter many species desert the uplands for the more hospitable lower altitudes. Whatever you do, remember to ensure you take plenty of warm clothing and a map, as even in summer the weather can be treacherous.

Freshwater lakes, rivers and gravel-pits

This can be one of the most interesting and productive habitats of all, especially if the water is surrounded by an area of trees and bushes, and is free from disturbance by watersports. Artificial habitats like disused gravel-pits are often just as good as natural ones, providing nesting habitat for Great Crested and Little Grebes, Sedge and Reed Warblers, Reed Bunting and specialities like the Little Ringed Plover. Rivers support their own special birds, including the Kingfisher and Grey Wagtail and, in the uplands, the Dipper.

Above The Dartford Warbler is a typical species of lowland heath in southern England. Mild winters have helped the population reach record levels.

Left The male Capercaillie is one of the most elusive and sought-after birds in Britain. It is confined to the Caledonian Pine Forests of the Scottish Highlands.

Time of year: A visit at most times of year should produce something of interest, with breeding birds throughout spring and summer, the chance of passage migrants such as terns during spring and autumn, and wintering ducks, cormorants and other waterfowl in winter. Large, man-made reservoirs hold vast numbers of wildfowl throughout autumn and winter.

Estuary and coastal marsh

Britain's coastal estuaries and marshes provide a rich source of food for many species of wader and wildfowl such as ducks, geese and swans. Remember that knowing the tide times is vital if you want to get close-up views, with a visit either side of high tide generally the most productive. In winter, this habitat also attracts predators such as the Peregrine, Merlin and Short-eared Owl. Bill gives a thrilling account of watching geese on the Dumbles estuary mudflats against a swiftly incoming tide (see page 157).

Time of year: The best season to visit is usually the winter months, when vast numbers of wildfowl and waders arrive from the north and east to enjoy the benefits of our milder winter climate, and ample food supplies. Spring and autumn passage periods can also be excellent, with large numbers of waders passing through on the way to and from their Arctic breeding-grounds and their winter quarters in Africa.

The sea

Perhaps you don't think of the sea as being a habitat at all – but in fact it supports a wide variety of birds. As well as coastal species like gulls and terns, the sea provides a rich feeding-ground for truly ocean-going species such as shearwaters and petrels. (See also Seawatching, page 98.)

Time of year: Spring and autumn see huge movements of seabirds past our coasts, including skuas and shearwaters, sea-duck like scoters and Eider, and auks such as the Guillemot and Razorbill. Timing is vital – the most productive seawatching is during bad weather and onshore winds. In winter, grebes and divers gather offshore, although they can often be difficult to identify in their drab non-breeding plumage (see page 23).

FIELDCRAFT: THE TOP TEN SKILLS YOU NEED TO ACQUIRE

As you explore all these wonderful new habitats, you'll begin to learn more about the way birds behave, particularly about how they react to your presence. Some birds don't seem to mind human beings at all, and will allow you to approach almost to within touching distance. Others will fly away as soon as they detect you, or are impossible to see because they seem to spend the whole time hidden in a reed-bed or dense forest canopy.

Birds are also, not surprisingly, suspicious of man. After all, for centuries we've hunted and killed them, stolen their eggs and destroyed their habitat. You can hardly expect them to let bygones be bygones and perform in front of you at the drop of a hat – anyway, birding wouldn't be half so enjoyable if they did!

This is where the birder's 'tricks of the trade' come in. Collectively, these are known as 'fieldcraft' – the skills you need to enable you to see birds better, without disturbing them or making them vulnerable to predators. Here, in no particular order, are the 'top ten' fieldcraft skills you should try to master:

1 Moving. Always move quietly and carefully – birds often react to movement by taking alarm. This is bad enough in most situations, but on a crowded estuary a sudden movement can result in a flock of thousands of birds taking fright and flying off.

2 Dressing. Avoid bright colours, spots, stripes and other bold patterns. What looks good on the High Street can send all kinds of wrong signals to a bird, so wear drab colours. Also avoid clothes that rustle – it's a dead giveaway!

3 Looking. It's amazing how unobservant some birders are. Perhaps it's because they spend all their time staring through binoculars instead of looking around them. So learn to look carefully, watching especially for those tiny movements that give away the presence of a bird, rather than a falling leaf!

4 Listening. Almost as important as looking. Birds often give away their presence by their voice. Sometimes this can mean a tiny, single, high-pitched note, almost too high for the human ear. So practise listening for these noises, then locating the birds. But remember, birds' calls are notoriously hard to fix direction on, so keep your eyes peeled.

5 Stalking. Once you've found a bird, you may need to get a closer view. So practise stalking on common birds, again moving carefully and deliberately, if necessary even crawling along the ground.

6 Clocking on. This is a great way to point out a bird you've found to a companion who hasn't seen it yet. Think of the direction dead in front of

The Merlin, our
smallest falcon,
breeds in upland
habitat, mainly in
northern Britain.
In winter, however,
it can often be
seen near the
coast.

you as twelve o'clock, to your right as three o'clock, and to your left as nine o'clock. Directions in between are ten, eleven, one and two o'clock. Use this to indicate the direction of the bird, but do make sure you're both looking in the same direction to start with!

7 **Whispering.** It's amazing how often you hear other birders before you see them. Some people just don't realize how loud their voice is – they must wonder why they don't see many birds. So try to communicate in a whisper – or at least talk quietly!

8 **Waiting.** A famous Scottish birdwatcher divided his colleagues into two camps: 'arsers' and 'leggers'. Of course, watching birds involves both skills, but we often spend much too much time moving, rather than sitting still and waiting. When you do, you'll be amazed what shows up – especially if you get yourself out of sight.

9 **Anticipating.** Wherever you are, you should always be thinking about what you might see next. Anticipation is one of the skills that comes with experience but, even so, you should have a reasonable idea of what to expect in a particular habitat or location.

10 **Enjoying.** It sounds obvious, but too many birders look as though they're having a thoroughly miserable time while they're out in the field. Above everything else, birding should be fun. As Bill always says, enjoy it!

CHOOSING AND USING A TELESCOPE

When you've been birding for a while, you may start to feel a little frustrated because birds don't always come close enough for you to see their plumage details through binoculars, and sometimes they're so far away you can't even identify them.

That's the time to dig deep in your pocket and splash out on a telescope. Telescopes, or 'scopes', as most birders call them, bring the birds a lot closer than binoculars, and used with a tripod, have the advantage of giving you a rock-steady image.

How telescopes work

Unlike binoculars, telescopes come in two sections:

- **The body,** with the large, objective lens at the front. Like binoculars, this is measured in millimetres, usually ranging from around 60mm to 80mm in diameter.

• **The eyepiece**, which fits on to the body by means of a 'bayonet' attachment, like a camera lens. The eyepiece can be either a fixed magnification (e.g. 20x or 30x) or a zoom (e.g. ranging in power from say 20x to 60x). Generally, fixed eyepieces are noticeably better quality than zoom ones and give a wider field of view.

Most scopes come with a '**straight**' eyepiece, in which your angle of view is in line with the body of the telescope. However, some models also come in an '**angled**' version, with the eyepiece at a 45° angle to the body. This can be especially useful for watching high-flying birds of prey. Generally, though, the straight version is the best, especially if you're new to using a scope.

Choosing a telescope

When choosing a telescope, there are three things to consider:

• **Power.** You might think that the higher the power, the better the scope – but as with binoculars (see page 12), this isn't necessarily the case. What you gain in power, you lose in clarity of image, brightness and field of view. Most birders prefer to use a 'wide-angle' eyepiece, such as a 20x WA or 30x WA. Never buy a scope with a single eyepiece greater than 30x magnification – the light is rarely strong enough for you to use it and, besides, the field of view will be far too narrow.

• **Weight.** Again, compromise is necessary. Some of the best and most powerful scopes are quite heavy and bulky, something you'll really notice after a long day in the field. You may prefer to go for a smaller, lightweight model, which can also take a lighter tripod. However, if you do so, you may have to make some sacrifices in quality.

• **Cost.** As with binoculars, there is an element of 'you get what you pay for' with scopes. If you have a limited budget, go for one of the smaller 'spotting scopes'. A reasonable scope-and-tripod combination starts at around £200, though you can pay well over £1000 for a top-of-the-range model. The extra cost buys you higher-quality lenses (those with a fluorite coating are the very best), and better build. Ideally you should buy the very best body you can afford, with a single, wide-angle eyepiece (probably a 20x WA). You can always buy extra eyepieces later on.

Before you buy a telescope, it's vital to **try out a range of models in the field.** Many of the specialist retailers who advertise in the monthly birding magazines (see page 216) hold regular field events at locations up and down the country, where prospective buyers can test out a variety of scopes and eyepieces under realistic conditions.

In particular, check the **sharpness of the image** (especially at the edges), the **field of view,** and how quickly and easily you can **focus.** If possible, compare different models side by side, and in poor light conditions, where differences in quality will be most apparent.

Finally, many scopes come with an optional 'stay-on' case, which protects the body from scratching and scuffing. If you're unlucky enough to drop your scope, it may also provide it with some degree of protection.

Tripods

You normally use a scope in conjunction with a tripod to keep it steady. Tripods come in all sizes and weights, and which one you choose is usually a matter of personal taste. Weight is important: if it's too light, the scope will shake in the wind; too heavy, and you won't enjoy carrying it long distances. Also, make sure that the tripod has 'quick-release' legs, to enable you to raise it to the full height as quickly as possible.

A tripod with a 'pan-and-tilt' fluid head will enable you to pan from left to right, tilt up and down, or pan and tilt at the same time, in any direction. This is particularly useful when following birds in flight.

You can also buy a variety of 'monopods', useful if you mainly use your scope in a hide, and 'car-pods', which attach the scope to your car window to enable you to use the car as a mobile hide.

Using a telescope

As with new binoculars (see page 15), using a telescope and tripod takes practice and patience. The best place to start is somewhere with a good, wide field of view and the continued presence of feeding or roosting birds, such as a reservoir, coastal marsh or estuary.

Practise the 'pan-and-scan' technique, adjusting the panning mechanism so it runs smoothly and easily, yet stays firm when you want to stop and look at a particular group of birds. Once you have mastered the technique, you'll soon be at ease.

The sight of a Kingfisher is guaranteed to brighten up a day's birding anywhere in the British Isles.

BIRDING WITH OTHERS

Birdwatching on your own can be fun and a challenge, but you may also want to join up with other like-minded souls to share your knowledge and learn new skills. You can do this in a number of ways.

Get yourself a mentor

When you're new to birding, it can be difficult trying to work out every-thing on your own. So why not get yourself a mentor – a more experienced birder who can help you identify birds, guide you round unfamiliar new habitats and answer the hundred-and-one questions you want to ask?

Ask your mentor to challenge your knowledge and test you on your growing skills in identification and fieldcraft. Hopefully it won't be long before you'll be able to teach him or her a thing or two!

But how do you find this ornithological mastermind? Maybe you already know someone who's been birding longer than you and can give you the benefit of their expertise. If not, why not...

Join your local bird club

Joining a local bird club or natural history society is a great way to meet other birders and develop your interest. Consult your local library for how to go about this. The RSPB also has a nationwide network and Members Groups.

Bird clubs usually cover a county or metropolitan area. Most publish an annual report of sightings, which is a useful way of finding out what you can expect to see in your local area, and can make fascinating reading.

Most clubs hold evening meetings, slideshows and so on, and also day trips to good birding spots in the local area and beyond. These are nor-mally by coach or shared car, so it's not usually a problem if you don't have your own transport.

Going on regular outings with a bird club is an ideal way to explore new places, with the advantage that being in a small group often gives you a better chance of finding good birds. You can also learn a lot from more experienced club members, though beware the 'club bore', who's usually a pretty lousy birder!

What's That Bird Doing?

An introduction to bird behaviour

As you watch birds more closely, and get to know the various different species, you soon start to wonder why they behave in the way they do. Why do birds sing? Why do they flock together at certain times of day or night? Why do some ducks dive while others dabble?

The study of bird (and animal) behaviour is known as ethology. Surprisingly, perhaps, it is a relatively young science, pioneered in the inter-war years by Niko Tinbergen and Konrad Lorenz. These men realized that the study of corpses in museums or cagebirds in zoos can only bring a limited understanding of how birds function. To really know how they tick, you need to watch them living their normal daily lives in the wild.

The great thing about studying bird behaviour is that anyone can do it, at least on a basic level. It can be done when and where you like, and even a complete amateur can discover something new or interesting. Also, it doesn't require any expensive or specialized equipment (apart from binoculars and a notebook).

It's worth getting into the habit of making notes about behaviour: not just odd or unusual things, but whatever catches your eye. In recent years, the obsession with bird identification has brought about something of a neglect in the study of bird behaviour, but now the tide may have turned, with many birders taking a greater interest in the way birds behave.

THE WAY BIRDS BEHAVE

Birds do all kinds of things in their day-to-day lives. Feeding or flying, roosting or flocking, swimming or diving are all aspects of bird behaviour. Of course, putting behaviour into different categories like this is a rather

This photograph, taken with high-speed flash photography, reveals the sheer beauty and elegance of the Barn Owl's flight.

artificial approach, as most types of behaviour occur as part of the business of day-to-day survival.

Nevertheless, it is useful to understand the basic reasons behind some of the commonest forms of behaviour. In this book we can only scratch the surface of this fascinating subject, but there are many excellent books on the behaviour of individual species or groups, or on specialized subjects like bird migration.

Flying

One of the most distinctive characteristics of birds is of course their ability to fly. This isn't unique – other animals, such as bats and insects, share this skill, and certain birds are flightless. But birds do have an excellent claim to be masters of the air.

Birds' bodies are well adapted to flight: they have hollow bones, powerful muscles to flap their wings, and feathers. Feathers are the perfect structure for getting and keeping airborne: light, strong and flexible, enabling birds to manoeuvre in mid-air, and undertake vast migratory journeys.

Birds fly in all kinds of ways: some flap, others soar or glide (often using thermal air currents), and many employ a combination of techniques depending on the circumstances.

Take time to look at different birds in flight: how they get airborne, whether they flap their wings or take advantage of air currents, and how they land. Watch whole groups of birds in flight, such as spectacular flocks of waders, turning as if controlled by a single mind. Finally, watch flying specialists like a hovering Kestrel, and marvel at their ability to control their position with tiny movements of the wings.

Feeding

Birds eat to live; or possibly live to eat; whichever way you put it, they spend an enormous proportion of their lives feeding or in search of food. For most of the year this is to sustain themselves, but during the spring and summer months they may have a family of hungry chicks to feed as well.

Many species of bird have developed specially-shaped bills to exploit one specific food source or habitat. So insectivorous warblers have thin, delicate bills, while seed-eating finches have thick, powerful bills. Perhaps the most specialized group are the waders, where different

Different bill shapes to suit different diets: the insect-eating warbler, the seed-eating finch and the hook-beaked bird of prey.

species have evolved different-length bills and legs to enable them to exploit particular foods and feeding areas.

Others, especially gulls and crows, can eat almost anything, and feed on whatever happens to be most easily available. These species tend to thrive especially on the products of human wastefulness.

Some birds, like the Blackcap, change their diet from summer to winter, replacing insects with a broader diet including fruit and scraps. Others do so only when cold weather forces them to, such as one Water Rail that took to killing and eating garden birds during one hard winter.

If you have a garden feeding-station, try noting down which species prefer which particular foods, and at what time of year. You may be surprised at what you find out.

Flocking and roosting

Birds come together in flocks for a whole variety of reasons, but the main ones are:

- **Food.** Flocks gather to exploit a plentiful food source, such as grain on a stubble-field, or the fertile mud of an estuary. In winter, many smaller species such as tits and finches form flocks, giving them a better chance of locating scarce food resources.
- **Safety.** There is safety in numbers, especially if there's a predator about. So waders and wildfowl will roost in vast flocks at high tide, while they wait for their feeding areas to become available again.
- **Warmth.** Especially during cold winter nights, small birds like Wrens or Pied Wagtails will huddle together in a communal roost to keep warm. Without this, any individual would stand a far lower chance of surviving the night.

At all times of the year, but especially outside the breeding season, certain species will come together as night falls, to go to roost. The most

Mallards are 'dabbling' ducks, named after their habit of feeding just below the water's surface.

spectacular and easily observed roosts are those of gulls on urban reservoirs, and Starlings, which often come into city centres to take advantage of the milder night-time temperatures there.

Flocking and roosting are a great asset to birders, as they enable you to locate particular species more easily, and often allow spectacular close-up views. High-tide wader roosts, consisting of a wide variety of different species, are especially interesting to watch.

Swimming and diving

Some birds don't just fly: indeed, they spend far more of their time swimming, and either dabbling or diving under the water for food. The best-known aquatic birds are ducks, geese and swans or, as they are collectively known, waterfowl. But other birds that habitually feed or roost on water include divers, grebes, shearwaters, cormorants, Coot and Moorhen, phalaropes, gulls and auks.

Some of these, such as the Coot and Moorhen, are exclusively fresh-water species, while others, like shearwaters and auks, are almost always found on the sea. But many species, including grebes and several species of duck, are equally adapted to fresh or salt water, though they generally feed in one or other habitat, and only visit the other to roost.

Ducks are one of the best groups for studying the way in which feeding requirements dictate behaviour. Some, like the Mallard and Shoveler, are 'dabblers', sifting the surface of the water or 'upending' for food. Others, like the Tufted Duck and Pochard, are 'divers', and as the name suggests, dive down under the water to the bottom of the lake or reservoir to obtain food there. In such cases, a bird's feeding technique can also be a useful pointer towards identifying the species.

Calls and song

As we saw in Chapter 2 (What's that Bird?) birds sing for two main reasons: to defend a territory against rival males of the same species and to attract a partner. So bird song is mainly a feature of spring, when male birds like the Blackcap begin to form territories in which they hope to find a mate (or mates), build a nest and raise their young. Male birds are notoriously prone to sneaking into another male's territory and trying to fertilize the female, so defending their territories is a deadly serious business.

For the human listener, bird song is a dazzling and often confusing mixture of sound: sometimes harsh, often beautiful. Some of our most famous singers, such as the Nightingale and Blackbird, are actually pretty dull-looking birds, whereas brighter species often have a less complex song.

There is a good evolutionary reason for this: birds able to attract a mate with their splendid plumage don't need such an advanced song, whereas birds that live most of their lives in woods and forests do, as they are heard more often than seen!

Not all birds sing exclusively in the breeding season: Robins also defend winter territories, and can often be heard in full song, brightening up a dull autumn or winter's day.

Bird calls are rather different: although they do occur in the breeding season, they are most commonly heard in the autumn and winter months. That's because for many small birds, the best way to locate sources of food is in a flock, kept together by constant 'contact calls'. This can be a good way to locate a flock of feeding tits in winter.

Another frequently heard form of call occurs when a bird is flushed (caused to take flight) or frightened: these 'alarm calls', warning fellow birds of danger, are common amongst waders such as the Redshank.

Courtship and breeding

Long before spring is in the air, sometimes even when snow is lying on the ground, a bird's thoughts turn to courtship and breeding. This is when things get serious, for if a bird fails to breed it may die before it gets another chance to pass on its genes to a new generation.

So, after feeding, courtship is the most important aspect of bird behaviour. It starts with pair formation, where a male bird approaches one or more females and tries to impress them with his song, plumage or other form of display. Watching this, you are witnessing the basic driving force of evolution, as each male tries to attract the healthiest-looking female, while the females compete to attract the finest male.

Not all succeed. In many species, there is a large proportion of non-breeders who have missed the boat for that particular season and spend the summer in flocks rather than pairs.

One of the easiest courtship rituals to observe is that of the Feral Pigeon. The male puffs himself up like a prizefighter, then performs a little dance around the female. After much bowing and scraping, the male will attempt to copulate with the female, though as often as not she will foil his amorous advances.

The most spectacular display commonly on view in the British Isles is that of the Great Crested Grebe, which can take place as early as January. The two birds face each other in the water, rubbing their bills together and shaking their heads in a ritual bonding. If you're really lucky, you may even see the memorable 'Penguin dance', during which both birds gather water-weed in their bills, then 'stand up' in the water, frantically paddling their legs to stay upright.

Nests, eggs and chicks

The next step after pair formation is to find a suitable site for a nest and begin building. Creating the right nest-site can be time-consuming; in the case of the Wren, the tiny male may build several nests before the choosy female agrees to lay her eggs in one of them.

Nests can be complex structures. They may be carefully constructed out of twigs, moss and feathers, or simply a hole in a tree lined with a few

bits of vegetation. Some are neat, like the Blackbird's nest; others are messy, like the heap of sticks thrown together by the Wood Pigeon. But all nests are there to serve the same purpose: to provide

A Coot's nest, made of twigs so that it floats but securely anchored so that it doesn't drift away. Coots often take over an old Grebe's nest and add more material.

a safe, secure home for the eggs and, for many species, the chicks as well.

Birds lay anything between one single egg, as in the case of many seabirds, and twenty or more, as do the Partridge and Pheasant. The majority of species has a single brood of chicks in a single season, but others may raise two or more sets of young.

If a nest is destroyed or the eggs are eaten by a predator, most pairs will attempt to breed again. Eggs are incubated for as little as eleven days, as in the case of small songbirds, to several weeks, as with many seabirds. They are usually incubated by the female, but sometimes by both parents or, in a few cases, solely by the male bird.

Once the chicks are hatched, they can be divided into two types. The young of songbirds such as the Blue Tit and Blackbird are born blind and without feathers (known as nidicolous or altricial young). In contrast, young ducks, waders and gamebirds are born in a relatively developed state and are able to leave the nest, run or swim almost immediately after hatching (they are known as nidifugous or precocial young).

BIRD MIGRATION
Why do birds migrate?

Question: Why do birds fly south in the autumn?
Answer: Because it's too far to walk!

It's a corny old children's riddle, but it raises a question that has baffled mankind for centuries. Why do birds migrate? What impels them to leave a comfortable home here in the British Isles and head south to spend the winter in sub-Saharan Africa, facing all kinds of hazards on their long journey? And once birds have actually reached their winter quarters, why don't they simply stay there? What drives them back again the following spring?

It has been estimated that more than 5 *billion* birds, of over 200 different species, undertake the twice-yearly journey between Eurasia and Africa. The traditional reason given for migration is that these birds are unable to survive the northern winter, and must head south to find food. While true, this is only half the story.

To regard Swallows, Swifts and Willow Warblers as 'our' birds, heading south for the winter, is the wrong way round. These birds originated in Africa and headed north to avoid competition with other species there. By travelling to the higher latitudes of the northern hemisphere, they found abundant food supplies, fewer competitors and longer hours of daylight in which to raise their young.

Migratory birds have developed all kinds of adaptations to enable them to survive the perils of migration. These include longer wings, the ability to store large amounts of fat as fuel and navigational skills.

Recent studies have revealed that migration may not be as hazardous as staying put for the winter, when snow and ice can cover up food supplies and bring rapid starvation and death. One migration expert has even turned the familiar question on its head: 'The question is often asked, "Why do birds migrate?" Rather, we should be surprised that there are some birds that are sedentary: why do not *all* birds migrate?'

As Bill points out on page 124, migration is a miracle. For him, and for many other birdwatchers, it is the single most thrilling aspect of birding. He gives an exhilarating account of watching birds migrate south from the top of Parliament Hill on Hampstead Heath (see page 145), and of a spectacular 'fall' of migrants on Fair Isle on page 197.

How do birds navigate?

For centuries, man has tried to discover how migrating birds navigate. All sorts of devices have been proposed, from the sun to the stars and from the earth's magnetic field to a highly developed sense of smell. So what is the answer?

In fact, scientists now believe that there is no single solution. Instead, birds appear to rely on a whole range of navigational aids, allowing migrants to avoid putting all their eggs in one basket, as it were. For example, a bird migrating at night (as do most songbirds) will normally use the stars to navigate; but when skies are cloudy it will turn to a different system to avoid getting lost.

Not all navigational aids are external; some are genetically programmed. Juvenile birds undertaking their first migratory journey in autumn rely on a fairly crude 'point-and-compass' method, similar to that used by early human sailors. Essentially, the bird is programmed to fly in a particular direction for a specific length of time. If it avoids any hazards it should, in theory at least, end up at its chosen destination. In practice, the system is prone to errors, explaining why so many young birds go astray each autumn, and fail to survive the migratory journey.

Vagrants and vagrancy

A vagrant is simply a bird that has, for whatever reason, wandered off course to end up in a place where it is not normally found. This generally happens during spring or autumn migration, although vagrants can and do turn up at every season of the year and in the most unlikely places.

The majority of vagrants is young birds, often on their first migratory journey. Because they use a fairly unsophisticated navigational system, they are at the mercy of changes in weather conditions. Crosswinds, in particular, can push a bird off its intended course.

The British Isles are extraordinarily well placed to receive vagrants from all four points of the compass – especially from the east and west. This goes a long way to explaining the popularity of 'twitching', in which the observer may travel long distances to see a particular rare bird (see page 96). People often wonder what happened to these wind-blown strays. It is likely that most, if not all, fail to find their way back home.

Autumn is the prime season for vagrants, with westerly gales bringing North-American waders and landbirds across the Atlantic to make land-fall in rarity 'hotspots' such as the Scilly Isles, Cornwall and also south-west Ireland.

On Britain's east coast, birdwatchers hope for high pressure over Siberia combined with rain and fog over the North Sea, which may bring birds like Yellow-browed and Pallas's Warblers to our shores. These tiny creatures should be sunning themselves in South-east Asia but, due to a mistake in their navigational mechanism, often end up thousands of miles astray in the British Isles. Sadly, most are ill-equipped to survive the British winter and soon perish.

Spring vagrants often include splendid singing male birds, which occa-sionally take up a territory in the hope that a female will join them. These are mainly migrants returning from Africa to southern Europe, which have 'overshot' their intended destination. This happens as a result of high pressure systems which bring fine weather across the Continent, and encourage the birds to continue their journeys northward to the British Isles.

How weather affects birds

As we have already seen, the weather has an enormous effect on migratory birds, often resulting in disorientation or even death. But the weather can have an equally major effect on our resident birds, especially in winter.

Thanks mainly to the warming influence of the Atlantic Ocean and its currents, our mild winter climate makes the British Isles a globally important wintering-ground for millions of waders, ducks, geese and swans. They arrive each autumn from their northern and

Swallows, House and Sand Martins gather together in flocks before heading south in autumn.

eastern breeding-grounds and then spend the winter months feeding and roosting on our coastal estuaries and mudflats.

They are joined here by many millions of songbirds from the Continent, for example, Skylarks, finches and thrushes, which also flee the harsher winters to the east. In the

meantime, many of our own birds head across the English Channel to spend the winter in France or Spain.

Even on a local scale you can often observe weather-related bird movement. On fine, sunny days in spring, watch for the first arrivals of summer visitors such as House Martins or Swifts, and listen out for returning warblers, whose song is usually the first indication that they have arrived. In autumn, early morning observations from a high watchpoint may bring a passage of thrushes, pipits or finches overhead, their presence only given away by high-pitched contact calls.

In winter, look out for the onset of harsh weather on the near Continent, which often drives birds like Redwings, Fieldfares and wild-fowl across the North Sea to take refuge here.

THE WIDER PICTURE

Bird populations and how they change

When you begin birdwatching, it's easy to assume that the birds you see are part of some static equilibrium, unchanged for centuries. In fact, bird populations and their range and distribution change very rapidly – well within the experience of a single human lifetime.

Perhaps the most famous example is the Collared Dove. Back in the 1930s, the nearest this attractive dove came to Britain was the Ural Mountains, more than 2000 miles away. For unknown reasons, the species began to head westwards, and was first recorded breeding in Britain in the early 1950s. Less than half a century later it is one of our most common and widespread birds, its monotonous cooing call a familiar part of the British landscape.

The Collared Dove is just one of more than a dozen species to have colonized the British Isles as a breeding bird for the first time this century. Meanwhile, birds like the Osprey and Avocet, victims of persecution and changes in land-use during the nineteenth century, have returned to breed here. Sadly, the same period has also seen the loss of a handful of British breeding birds, including the Kentish Plover and most recently the Red-backed Shrike.

The last decade or so has brought alarming news about some of our commonest birds, with the Skylark and Song Thrush, amongst others, experiencing rapid and major population declines. This is mainly due to the spread of modern agricultural methods, which must be reversed if these species are to regain their former status.

Not all of man's influence has been so harmful to birds. A century ago, the presence of gulls inland in winter was almost unknown; today, millions spend the winter in our towns and cities and recently some birds have even stayed on to breed there, taking advantage of the abundant supplies of waste food we provide.

Now, more than ever, ordinary birdwatchers can contribute to our knowledge of these rapid changes in bird populations, either by participating in official surveys (see Chapter 6), or simply by keeping detailed notes on the numbers of birds in their local area.

Bird protection and conservation

Birdwatching and the protection and conservation of birds have always gone hand-in-hand. The RSPB was originally founded more than a century ago by a group of Victorian women protesting against the use of bird feathers as fashion accessories. Today it is Europe's largest voluntary conservation organization, and the views of its million members carry considerable weight.

Sometimes individual birders get frustrated at events and policies, like the encouragement of intensive agriculture through farm subsidies, which they know will lead to the decline of birds, both locally and nationally. However, with environmental issues taking an ever greater place at the centre stage of politics, future prospects may be better.

As we approach the new millennium, birders are faced with a choice. We can simply enjoy our hobby, or we can join together to influence conservation organizations and local and national government to protect birds and their habitats. So join the RSPB, the BTO (see page 214) and your local Natural History Society and help protect and conserve our birdlife for generations to come. After all, if we don't look after our birds, no one else will.

Bird names

What's in a name? When it comes to birds, quite a lot. For a start, birds don't just have one name: as well as their common name, they may have an 'official' name, various local folk-names and in every case a 'scientific' name unique to that particular species.

Take the Mistle Thrush (or Missel Thrush, as it is sometimes spelt). This handsome bird used to be called a Throstle (a name shared with its smaller cousin the Song Thrush); in country areas it's known as the Stormcock, due to its habit of singing before and during a thunderstorm; it has at least half-a-dozen obsolete folk-names; and is known to ornithologists the world over as *Turdus viscivorus*.

Confused? You needn't be! Most British species are known by one main English name, with perhaps one or two less widely used folk-names, and the scientific name, which should always be referred to in the case of doubt, as it is less liable to change than the English one.

Above The Golden Oriole has only recently colonized Britain as a breeding bird, with a small but growing population in East Anglia and south-east England.

Right The Red-backed Shrike, once a familiar sight in rural England, is now extinct as a British breeding bird.

English names

But where do bird names come from? Why are some birds named after people (*Bewick's* Swan) and others after places (*Dartford* Warbler)? Why are some named by where they live (*Marsh* Tit), some by their size (*Great* Tit) and others by their colour (*Blue* Tit)? Why are many species of birds named after their call (*Chiffchaff, Kittiwake*), but not after their smell?!

The reason is that most birds were named by the people who first watched them and realized they were a distinct species. So it's hardly surprising that many birds are named after either an obvious plumage feature (Red-throated Diver, Great Crested Grebe), their size (a whole host of Littles, Lessers and Greaters), their habitat (Tree, Willow, Marsh and so on) or perhaps, most often, after their sound.

The best-known onomatopoeic bird-names are Cuckoo, Chiffchaff and Kittiwake. But scratch the surface of many other names and you'll find a reference to the bird's call. Our ancestors called the Chaffinch 'Pink' or 'Spink' because of its distinctive flight-call. Over the centuries, this gradually changed into the word 'finch'. Rook, Crow, Raven and even Turtle (as in Turtle Dove) are also derived from the birds' calls.

But not all bird names are so easy to understand. Some are positively misleading. Wheatears have nothing to do with 'ears of wheat' – the name literally means 'White-Arse', and goes back to the days when 'arse' had no vulgar connotations and simply meant 'rump'.

For a newcomer to birdwatching, learning the names of birds can be a real headache. There just doesn't seem to be any consistency! After all, why do most birds in the warbler family have the word 'warbler' in their name, yet other species of the same family, such as the Whitethroat, Blackcap and Chiffchaff, do not? Surely it would be more logical to standardize the names and avoid confusion?

Well, it's a nice idea and, like modernizing English spelling, one that's been around for a long time. But although reform has been attempted several times, most recently by the eminent members of the British Ornithologists' Union, the new names just don't seem to catch on. After all, who wants to call Shelley's Skylark a Sky Lark, just because a committee says so!

Of course, bird names are far from permanent. Pick up any Victorian bird book and you'll find references to the Willow-Wren (Willow Warbler) and Golden-crested Wren (Goldcrest). These names fell out of use

WHAT'S THAT BIRD DOING? **87**

because they were misleading – rather in the way Hedge Sparrow has recently been superseded by Dunnock. But any future changes are likely to be equally gradual, taking tens of years rather than one or two.

Scientific names

Every bird in the world, apart from one or two that haven't been discovered yet, has a scientific name – or rather, two scientific names. The system was invented by the great Swedish botanist Linnaeus, way back in the eighteenth century. Linnaeus developed a simple system called 'binomial nomenclature' – which just means 'giving two names'. The first, or generic name, denotes the genus and is shared with other close relatives; the second, or specific name, denotes the particular species being described.

Thus he gave the Chaffinch the scientific name *Fringilla coelebs*. It shares the generic name *Fringilla* with the Brambling, demonstrating their close relationship compared with other finches; while the specific name *coelebs* derives from the Latin for bachelor. Linnaeus chose this curious name because in his native Sweden, only male Chaffinches remain for the winter, while females and juveniles migrate farther south.

The beauty of scientific names is that just two words can distinguish between every single one of the world's 9000 or so different species of bird. This is clearly not the case with vernacular names, where confusion can occur, either when two different species share the same name (as in the New and Old World species of Black Vulture), or when one familiar species lacks a qualifying adjective, as in the Swallow, Wheatear and Cuckoo.

The system is also flexible. When a new species is discovered, or an existing one is 'split' into two or more species (as with Rock and Water Pipits), new scientific names are coined to distinguish between them.

You may wonder why you need to bother knowing these scientific names at all. In fact there are two good reasons. First, they provide a fascinating insight into relationships between different species and how they were named. The second reason is more practical: as you travel farther afield, where you don't share a common language with the locals, scientific names allow you to clarify which species you're talking about and help prevent confusion.

Overleaf Seabird city. A 'wall' full of Kittiwakes – everyone calling its name.

6 SPREADING YOUR WINGS

The great thing about watching birds is that you can do it on many different levels: from odd trips to the local park to full-scale expeditions to places like the Galapagos Islands, Kenya or even Antarctica! For Bill's advice on birding holidays and birding abroad, see chapter 10.

If you prefer to stay closer to home, you can broaden your experience and gain a greater depth of knowledge of birds by taking up a more specialized interest such as bird photography, ringing, or participating in bird surveys. In this chapter, we look at some of these activities and suggest ways of getting the most from them.

BIRD SURVEYS

How do we know which is the commonest bird in Britain? Or whether Skylarks are declining as a breeding bird? Or how many ducks, geese and swans spend the winter in the British Isles?

The answers to these, and many other questions, come from surveys – mainly those carried out by ordinary birdwatchers in their spare time. Of course, we can never get absolutely precise answers, but what surveys do provide is the raw material to detect rises and falls in population, changes in distribution and unusual events.

Take the Whitethroat population crash of 1969. One of our commonest summer migrants, the Whitethroat, spends the winter in western Africa. When more than four-fifths of Whitethroats failed to return to breed in the spring of 1969, birdwatchers all over Britain alerted the British Trust for Ornithology. The BTO collected details from all over the country, leading to the discovery that a widespread and severe drought in the Sahel Zone, where the birds spent the winter, was responsible for the massive decline.

Closer to home, recent surveys have shown declines in the populations of some of our commonest birds, such as the Song Thrush, Skylark and even the humble House Sparrow.

Some bird surveys are regular and continuous, such as the BTO's Breeding Bird Survey, or their Garden BirdWatch, which has more than 7000 participants. Others only take place from time to time, like the nationwide Atlas surveys that tell us about changes in breeding and wintering distribution. Finally, there are specialized surveys designed to monitor regularly the population of a single species, such as the Rook, Lapwing or Barn Owl, or a group, like seabirds or wildfowl.

You don't need to be an expert to take part in bird surveys. You do need some spare time and plenty of enthusiasm. Remember that you will be under the supervision of an experienced ornithologist, who will help you gain the skills and experience to contribute to survey work. Contact the BTO for further details of how you can take part and gain the satisfaction of putting something back into conserving Britain's birdlife (see Useful Addresses, page 214).

BIRD-RINGING

Ever since the Greeks tied coloured threads around the legs of migrating Swallows to find out where they spent the winter, man has practised some form of marking or ringing birds. At its most basic level, this enables the birdwatcher to pick out individuals from a flock; in its wider form, ringing enables us to track the global movements and migrations of birds.

In the United Kingdom, ringing is carried out under the supervision of the BTO. It is a highly skilled activity, with only around 1000 or so fully-qualified ringers in the whole country.

To be ringed in the first place, birds must be trapped. This is done in a variety of ways, including large permanent traps at bird observatories, but most birds are caught in 'mist-nets' – fine mesh nets placed in between bushes and trees, where birds will become entangled as they fly past.

Once the bird has been trapped, ringers normally weigh it, note down details of its age and sex (if known) and place a small metal ring around its leg. Each ring has its own unique number, together with the address of where to send it, should anyone 'recover' the bird, either by retrapping it or finding it dead.

Most birds are never recovered, but because so many thousands of birds have been ringed over the years, we have plenty of data on our common species. These figures are then analysed to provide information on short- and long-distance movements, how long birds live and the commonest causes of death.

Becoming a ringer is not something to undertake half-heartedly. It requires a long apprenticeship (typically around five years), and plenty of

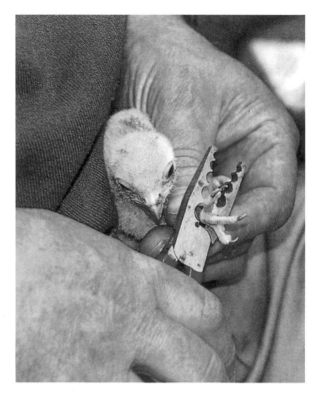

Left The Whitethroat, whose population crash caused by drought in Africa was confirmed by bird surveys.

Right Ringing birds teaches us a lot about how they live their lives.

time spent in the chilly early mornings catching birds. However, the rewards are enormous, and the knowledge and excitement to be gained from examining birds in the hand are well worth the effort.

If you want to witness bird-ringing without taking part yourself, there are several bird observatories which carry out regular ringing demonstrations. Contact the Ringing Unit at the BTO for further details (see Useful Addresses, page 214).

PHOTOGRAPHING BIRDS

One of the commonest questions asked of every birdwatcher is 'Do you photograph the birds you see?' It's almost as if people can't understand why you would want to watch birds if you couldn't keep a permanent visual record.

In fact, although many birders dabble in photography, very few take it up seriously. One reason is that the extra equipment is not only an added expense, but also doubles the weight you have to carry in the field. The main deterrent, however, is that when you photograph birds you often have to spend long periods of time in one place, waiting for a single bird to come close enough to capture on camera. So to get one decent photo may take all day, during which you don't get much opportunity to watch any other birds!

Nevertheless, bird photography is a fascinating pastime in its own right, and even on a part-time basis can enhance your birdwatching skills and knowledge.

Starting off

As with all new skills, photographing birds takes time and patience. So it's best to start by spending a couple of hours in a place where the birds come reasonably close. You might try your local park, where ducks, coots and gulls can be attracted by the provision of food. Or why not 'cheat', and visit a collection of birds such as those at many Wildfowl and Wetlands Trust Centres? You should be able to get close enough to take some really excellent pictures.

Use a longer lens than normal. If you're photographing captive birds, or those used to human presence, then something around 135-200mm will do. But if you want to photograph wild birds, such as those that visit your garden feeding-station, you probably need a 400mm or 500mm, ideally a good-quality one with a wide aperture.

Birds move very fast, so pick a bright day, set your ISO to 800, and mount your camera on a tripod to avoid shake. Use the fastest shutter-speed possible, and remember that although a bird can look quite near through the viewfinder you may be disappointed when the finished picture shows a tiny dot in the centre of the frame!

Branching out

If, having tried it out, you get serious about bird photography, then seek advice from an experienced practitioner. You'll also need to consider how much you want to invest: with camera equipment, the sky's the limit.

Digital cameras with ever-faster speeds and higher quality images enable even the beginner to take pretty impressive images. You may then want to play around with them using special software, but if you want to publish them in a book or magazine always let the editor know you have done so.

New developments in lenses, including image-stabilising technology, now allow you to hand-hold telephoto lenses even at quite slow shutter speeds; a real boon when on the move. But a good, sturdy tripod is also essential for really high quality results.

It's also worth considering going on a course in the basics of photography. These can be held at residential centres, such as those run by the Field Studies Council, or at your local Further Education Office. If you can find one that specializes in bird or nature photography, all the better.

Finally, remember that bird photography is expensive and requires a lot more dedication than simply watching birds. Some highly skilled and dedicated people do manage to make a living from it but, to begin with at any rate, don't give up the day job!

DRAWING AND PAINTING BIRDS

Every birdwatcher should have at least a basic knowledge of how to draw a field sketch as part of his or her field notes (see page 27). But some go further than this, and learn to draw and paint birds to a highly skilled level.

Obviously it helps to have some innate artistic ability, but practice and persistence are just as important. Several of today's professional bird artists began by sketching in their field notebook, and at least one supported his twitching expenses by selling portraits of the bird he'd come to see!

As with photography, it helps to get expert tuition. The Field Studies Council and other organizations run residential courses on drawing and painting (see Useful Addresses, page 214, for details), which will help you develop your skills. Whether you simply want to learn for your own pleasure and enjoyment, or you have ambitions to become a professional artist, it's a skill well worth acquiring.

SPECIALIZED BIRDING

Just as anglers fall into several camps, from coarse-fishing to fly-fishing, and sharks to salmon, so birdwatchers sometimes specialize in one particular area. Generally, it's best to acquire a broad range of skills and experience before taking up any of the following activities, but there's nothing to stop you dabbling – and who knows, you may even become hooked...

Twitching

If you tell someone you enjoy watching birds, chances are that the response will be, 'So you're a twitcher, then?' In recent years, the word 'twitching' has become synonymous with birdwatching, though the two are in fact quite different activities.

In one sense, any birder who travels to see a particular kind of bird is a twitcher. So if you're planning to visit Minsmere to see Avocets, or Loch Garten to watch the Ospreys, you're twitching. But in the true sense, a twitcher is someone who travels long distances especially to see an individual rare bird or vagrant. These global wanderers have often been blown thousands of miles off course while on migration to turn up on our shores, far from their intended destination.

The name twitcher has several possible derivations. It's often said that it was because early twitchers shivered with cold while waiting for a

rarity to turn up, but the more likely explanation is that it refers to a well-known birder back in the 1960s, who would literally twitch with excitement when he heard news of a rare bird.

Twitching has had its share of bad press, some of it deserved (see Bill's reservations about twitching taken to extremes, page 183). After all, there's nothing very environmentally-friendly about breaking the speed limit just to get to a rare bird more quickly, and cases of trespassing, crop-trampling and verbal abuse have been known.

Generally, though, twitchers are very keen birders, and often very skilled and knowledgeable too. They've also done a lot to change their negative image by making collections for conservation at major twitches.

Waiting for an Oriental Pratincole to appear over a Norfolk field...

If you want to try twitching, you can find out which rare birds are

present, and the directions to find them, by dialling a national phoneline, Birdline, on 09068 700222 (calls are charged at the premium rate).

If you don't want to travel such long distances, there are also regional birdlines covering various parts of the British Isles (details in monthly birding magazines, see page 216). You may get really keen, in which case you can even hire yourself a pager and get up-to-the-minute information on rare birds, wherever you are.

Seawatching

It has been said that seawatching is a bit like going to war: long periods of boredom and discomfort interrupted by moments of great excitement.

Seawatching is often just that: spending long periods staring at a grey, featureless stretch of water, while trying to stay awake and prevent frost-bite in your fingers and toes. The idea is to catch a glimpse of passing seabirds – and we're not talking common-or-garden gulls, but true seabirds like petrels, shearwaters and skuas.

Generally, these ocean-going species don't venture very near the coast. But there's one exception to this: in bad weather, they may pass close inshore in their thousands. The trouble is that when this happens the wind and rain often prevent you seeing them at all!

Most seawatching takes place during the spring and autumn migration periods, generally from a coastal promonotory such as Dungeness in Kent, Flamborough Head in Yorkshire, or one of the Cornish headlands. Seawatching is highly weather-dependent, usually requiring strong onshore winds and the passing of a weather front. It's best to seek advice on place, time and ideal conditions from an old hand, otherwise you may find yourself staring out to sea for long, birdless periods.

However, there is one way to cheat at seawatching: go on what birders call a 'pelagic'. Pelagics are trips on a boat out into the open sea, on the principle that it's easier for us to go to the birds than to wait for the birds to come to us. Pelagics can provide spectacular close-up views of species rarely seen close to the shore, and are often a memorable experience. However, they can also provide close-up views of the contents of your stomach, as the voyages often coincide with bad weather.

If you still want to go on a pelagic, look for the adverts in birding magazines, or for a more civilized way to get to grips with rare seabirds, contact the RSPB for details of their offshore 'cruises', which run off the Yorkshire coast every autumn.

BIRDING ABROAD

Once you've been watching birds for a while in the British Isles, you may want to see what's on offer elsewhere. Maybe it's all those natural history films on TV or the colour illustrations in the field guides, but there's something very tempting about travelling abroad in search of new and exotic species.

But where should you go for your first foreign trip? It makes sense to try a destination where at least some of the birds will be familiar, such as France, the Netherlands or a Mediterranean island.

Birds like the Hoopoe, a rare visitor to Britain, are commonplace over much of continental Europe, and most areas have their own speciality species, such as Eleonora's Falcon and Audouin's Gull in Mallorca, or Cyprus Warbler and Cyprus Pied Wheatear in – you've guessed it – Cyprus.

Birding on holiday with family or friends

If you've only got a couple of weeks' holiday a year, you may not be very popular with members of your family if you go off on your own on a specialist birding holiday.

Fortunately, you don't really need to. Some of the best birding in Europe can be had on the doorstep of popular holiday resorts like the Spanish costas, the Algarve in Portugal or the islands of Mallorca, Crete and Cyprus. Spring or autumn are the best times to visit, as these coincide with the peak migration seasons, but even in mid-summer there will always be some interesting birds.

If you're with family or friends, try not to spend the entire time staring through a pair of binoculars. Early morning and evening are usually the best times to watch birds, so devote these to birding and spend the rest of the time doing other things. By the end of the holiday you should find you've totted up an impressive list of species and gained valuable experience of birds rarely seen at home. For Bill's pointers towards enjoying birdwatching on a family holiday, see pages 205–211, at the end of the chapter in which he describes how he had some unexpected birdwatching experiences while on holiday with his wife and daughter at Disney World!

Organized bird tours

Although you can go birding abroad on your own, one of the best ways to do so is with an organized bird tour – preferably run by one of the specialist bird holiday companies. These may look expensive at first, but remember that the price generally includes everything except drinks, and you also get the benefit of expert leadership.

This means that within a week or ten-day-long tour you should manage to see most of a region's speciality species and more importantly get really good views. You'll also gain the benefit of being with expert birders, and meet other like-minded enthusiasts.

Organized bird tours abroad range from a few days in western Europe, starting at around £700, to four weeks in Antarctica, for upwards of £5000. Just reading the catalogues produced by these companies can be a mouth-watering experience, and actually going on a tour can truly be the experience of a lifetime.

Site reports and 'where to watch' guides

If you're travelling with your family or on your own, how do you find out what you're likely to see? Your first port of call is the various 'where to watch' guides, of which several now cover individual countries, such as France, or groups of countries, like eastern Europe or Spain and Portugal. These offer a good general introduction to the birds you may encounter, and also give information about specific sites in a particular area.

Even better are the private trip reports you can find online, produced by birders who have already visited your chosen destination. These are often really detailed, and may Inclued contact details for the authors so you can get in touch to discuss any species you particularly want to see.

Writing your own trip report

Birdwatching abroad is always a memorable experience, and when you return it's worth spending some time and effort writing up your sightings. This isn't just for your own benefit – a trip report can also be useful to anyone else who plans to visit the same area in the future.

A good trip report should include the following:

- **Dates** of your visit.
- A note on **weather conditions.**
- A list of **birding participants.**
- The **locations** you visited (with **site directions and maps** if possible).

- A **systematic list** of the birds you saw: with dates, times (where relevant), numbers of birds, etc.

Bee-eaters are one of the exotic species found near holiday destinations around the Mediterranean.

- **Field notes** for particular species: especially birds you haven't seen before, local rarities, or unusual plumages, behaviour, etc.
- **Line drawings** and/or **photographs** if you have them.
- Your **contact name, address and telephone number** for anyone who requires further information.

THE PRACTICE

7 LOCAL PATCH...

a year on Hampstead Heath

There are certain famous open spaces around the country that most people have probably heard of. For example, Sherwood Forest, Romney Marsh, Clapham Common and... Hampstead Heath. These days not many of them would stand up to examination by the Trades Description Board. Most of the natural habitats that gave them their names have long gone. Trees have been felled, wetlands have been drained, playing fields marked out, housing estates built, and so on. Certainly, there's not a lot of heathland left anywhere in the country, let alone in Hampstead. But at least Hampstead Heath still exists. To different Londoners it is the venue for different activities. Funfairs at Bank Holidays, cross-country runs in the winter, open-air concerts in summer, kite flying, jogging and dog-walking all year round. It even hits the headlines now and again when some pagan cult sets fire to a cross on top of Parliament Hill or a junior minister is caught lurking in the bushes in a compromising liaison. Yes, there's a lot going on out there and the truth is there's plenty of room for it. Hampstead Heath is still an open space and the Corporation of London, which manages it, is quite proud of it. The official guide book reads:

> *Hampstead Heath is a gloriously varied, irregular grouping of heathland, woodland, fields and formal grounds. Its 792 acres... form London's largest and loftiest open space. Upwards of four million people a year visit it, seeking its breezy uplands, secluded dells, leafy avenues and winding paths.*

...And its birds. There are, of course, birds on the Heath. The problem is finding them in those 792 acres, amongst those masses of people, especially when only three of the four million visitors are regular bird-watchers. I'm one of them. Hampstead Heath is my local patch.

Now and again, other people do wander around the Heath with binoculars – and some of them may even be birdwatching! – but, like I said, there really are, to my knowledge, only three of us who are devoted – nay, obsessed – regulars.

Peter is in his late sixties. (He may even be seventy by now.) He's been birding on the Heath for many, many years on and off and therefore knows the satisfaction – and the frustration – of being able to remember how it used to be. He has seen many changes, not many of them for the good. Now that he's retired, he can theoretically get out every day. During some seasons he does just that, albeit at a fairly leisurely pace. He admits his hearing isn't quite what it was, and I've suspected that he may be prone to occasional day-dreaming. Who can blame him? In any case, no one can be totally alert 100 per cent of the time. Inevitably, though, Peter sees a lot of birds.

Mark is younger – thirty-something probably. He is also 'something in the City', which means that he works all week and is also often called abroad on mysterious financial quests which we don't ask about. It means that his Heath visits are more sporadic than Peter's, but probably twice as intense. Considering he doesn't get out all that often, Mark finds an awful lot of good birds. This is no doubt a) because he tries that much harder and b) because he's an absolutely top-notch birder. Indeed, Mark represents what I personally think is the logical and ideal balance of ornithological interests – the complete, all-round birdwatcher if you like. He enjoys the occasional twitch for a rarity, he organizes at least one trip abroad each year and one British-based birding holiday, yet he retains his enthusiasm for local patch-watching. What's more, he shares his knowledge in all sorts of practical ways: by editing annual bird reports – not only for the Heath but also for the London Natural History society – by leading beginners' groups on nature walks, and by representing birds' interests on various management committees. Come to think of it, it's no wonder he's not got a family! Anyway, the point that I'm making is whatever your style of birding, don't just keep it to yourself. Make your records available and get involved in conservation issues. And I guarantee you'll find it more satisfying. Above all, though, enjoy it. Mark certainly enjoys the Heath, albeit it's rarely more often than at weekends.

And finally, there's me. Being freelance – a euphemism for 'not always employed'! – my time is fairly flexible. I don't get out as often as Peter, but probably slightly more often than Mark.

THE CIRCUIT

All in all, then, between the three of us, we've got Hampstead Heath pretty well covered. Or have we? The fact is that it's quite a big place;

London – the view from Parliament Hill.

792 acres did they say? I never can envisage an acre. All I do know is the Heath is flippin' enormous. There is no way that three of us could cover it fully, even if we split up, which we wouldn't dare to do, in case one of us saw something good and the others missed it! Sometimes I rather envy birdwatchers who cover a relatively small patch. There is something pleasantly controllable about having boundaries.

In our case we've had to sort of draw our own. Peter, Mark and I – whether we are on our own or together – tend to cover more or less the same route. I suppose it has partially evolved over a period of time and is based on the places where we've seen the best birds. It also covers a manageable distance. At a gentle walking pace the circuit would probably take about two hours (though if there's lots of birdy distractions it could take five or six!). This element of a regular routine is one of the most satisfying features of patch-watching. For a start, it rapidly gives shape and meaning to your records, and you soon become aware of fluctuations: birds that come and go, birds that are 'always there'. It is only by being conscious of what you expect to see that you fully appreciate the unexpected. With each visit your knowledge increases. You learn by experience which parts of your patch are particularly good for

which birds and this dictates your regular route. For example... on Hampstead Heath.

The Hill

We invariably start on top of Parliament Hill. This is one of the highest points in London, and it's worth going there for the view alone. Admittedly at weekends you are likely to get sawn in half by wayward kites or flying frisbees, but go there early and often enough and you begin to appreciate that no two sunrises are the same. Some days the city below looms almost menacingly from the mist, other mornings it basks in a golden glow. But, whatever the weather, you definitely feel up there above it all. A bird's-eye view, in fact. And that's exactly the point. Any high place, especially above an urban sprawl, is likely to be a good look-out point for seeing birds that are flying over. Not only is there a wide uninterrupted vista but also, because you are high up, you are closer to the height the birds are flying. You need good eyes and sharp ears, but it can be very exciting at times of migration. Many birds migrate at night, but when migration occurs during the day it is very visible, often on a spectacular scale with huge flocks of birds purposefully heading in the same direction. So that's how we start our Heath circuit: on top of the hill hoping for some 'vis mig'.

The Hedges

As well as looking out for birds flying over, we have a view of playing fields and a couple of small ponds, so if anything lands on those we should see it. Also, just behind us, is what we call First Hedge. Not a very novel name I know but, like all local patchers, we have given each and every area an agreed name or number, and the imagination soon wanes. The few hedges on the Heath are left over from a long-gone time when it was actually farmland. They are quite thick – except for the bits where dog-walkers have got their hounds to chew a way through rather than go round – and you only have to imagine yourself as a tired migrant flying across London to speculate that birds must appreciate the cover they provide.

After an hour or two of 'vis mig' watching, we are usually frozen to the spot 'cos there were no birds overhead; or we've got chronic neckache 'cos there were birds; or we're getting embarrassed by young ladies in leotards contorting themselves into slightly tempting postures during

their morning workouts; or we can't hear ourselves think for the boogie boxers returning from an all-night rave... or whatever. The fact is that as the sun climbs higher, so do many Londoners, and the

Above Sunrise over Parliament Hill. No, it's not me!
Right The Second Hedge. Now with several mature trees in it.

top of Parliament Hill tends to get a bit crowded. So that's the point when we hit the hedges.

First Hedge is followed by – you guessed it – Second Hedge. This, like First Hedge, has a variety of trees in it, and certain bits seem to be particularly attractive to certain species. Down the bottom end is a brambly section with nearby thistles that is the only place on the whole Heath that has a more or less permanent pack of House Sparrows, usually with a few attendant Greenfinches. A hundred yards up the hedge are two large dead trees – ex-elms no doubt – much beloved of woodpeckers, and fifty yards beyond that is an elderberry that entices Blackcaps in autumn and – very occasionally – Ring Ousels in spring. Then a couple of paths slice through the hedge, and beyond them is an extra bit, which we always used to ignore until, one August day, no fewer than three Redstarts flitted along it. They had been disturbed by a rambling dog, and that's the main problem with the Second Hedge. A traditional pooch path leads right up alongside it, so birds don't tend to stay long.

The Third Hedge has no such path. I have nothing against doggies, you understand, but it is surely not a coincidence that the Third Hedge is consistently the most productive line of cover on the Heath. It is also in a dip and therefore usually sheltered from the wind and the calmest, tangliest part of it also faces east and is thus lit up by the morning sun, which brings out the insects and – with any luck – the birds. There is also an excellent mix of bird-friendly foliage: hawthorns, elders and alders, blackberries, oaks and sycamores. Actually, come to think of it, it's not

just because it's a dog-free zone that the Third Hedge is so good. Be honest, we might have designed it specially for birds – and indeed bird-watchers. There is even a lone tree, which stands separate from the hedge, with a bench just above it where we can sit and wait for the migrants to flit out and give us a better view.

Among the three main hedges there are large grassy areas. These used to be kept pretty manicured but, in recent years, thanks to an enlightened policy by the Corporation, they have been left to grow much wilder. To be honest, I don't think it has made much difference to the bird life, but the increase in flowers and butterflies has made it all look much less park-like. This area is dotted with benches, which we always scan as they provide convenient perches for Wheatears in spring.

Highgate Ponds

The next phase of the circuit involves checking the Highgate Ponds. There are several of them, one after another, along a valley (presumably once a river). None of the ponds is very big and each has a path along at least one side. In truth, we three birders often fantasize about creeping out at night with a large bulldozer and merging all the little ponds into one long lake and, whilst we're at it, ploughing up the paths and putting a fence around the lot. No doubt this would increase the bird life, but possibly not as much as we might imagine. The fact is that even small ponds can attract wildfowl and waders now and then, as long as they are in the right place. I used to watch a couple of glorified puddles just outside Birmingham which must have been along some kind of flyway because lots of good birds dropped in, even if they didn't stay very long. This doesn't happen at Highgate, but each pond has its own character, and a few of its own birds.

First Highgate Pond (another imaginative name!) is a bit of a contra-diction in management terms. Three sides of it are pretty inaccessible, protected by fencing and with some natural vegetation, including over-hanging willows. In the middle of the pond are three floating wooden platforms, put there specially for ducks or geese to nest on. So, all in all, the signs are that the pond is meant mainly for wildlife. It's an irony – and a pity – that the fourth bank of the pond has a path running along it, right by the water's edge which, because this is the first pond that dog-walkers come to, acts as a launching pad from which sticks are hurled into the water with assorted hounds in flying pursuit. Naturally, the dogs soon discover that it is more fun chasing ducks and geese than sticks. Nevertheless, a few birds do still attempt to breed there, and in winter the rafts provide loafing and preening perches for gulls and Cormorants.

The second Highgate Pond is the Men's Bathing Pond, or 'Masochist's Mere' as it perhaps deserves to be christened, since hardy males hurl themselves into it every morning and every season, even if they have to break the ice. Much as I admire them, I do feel slightly resentful that the lake is thus rendered almost permanently birdless.

So, on to the Model Boating Pond. This one might have been designed to deter birds. The sides are concrete, and there is a gravel path all round it. And – just to make sure – every now and then model boat enthusiasts launch demented little remote-controlled craft which tazz round, apparently remotely completely uncontrolled, making a noise that would drown out a Harley Davidson. And yet – perverse little blighters that birds are – the ducks seem to love it. This is consistently the only pond on the Heath that supports a decent array of wildfowl and a pair of Great Crested Grebes that nest so close to the bank that they can be photographed with a standard lens. In appreciation of the pleasure the birds give to passers-by the Corporation has rigged up a line of floats to ward off the model boats.

Nevertheless, how or why the wildfowl put up with the Boating Pond I do not know, any more than I can understand why they shun the Sanctuary Pond, which is just across the path. As its name implies, this one is entirely fenced off and designated as a Nature Reserve. There is a small reed-bed with nesting Reed Warblers in it, but ducks rarely dabble or dive on the placid waters. Nevertheless, it's very pretty and the willows are always worth checking for other warblers, or maybe the odd Reed Bunting.

The penultimate pond in the Highgate valley is the Ladies' Bathing Pond. It is entirely shrouded by fences, and it goes without saying that lurking around there with binoculars will get you arrested! So we don't. Instead, we quickly check the Stock Pond, which was presumably once used to rear fish. Not any more, as its almost invariable birdlessness testifies. Even so, it too has its specialities: if ever a Mandarin Duck turns up on the Heath, it's usually sleeping in the shadows alongside the Stock Pond, and the feeder stream never freezes even in the coldest weather, and is consequently a good place to see the Water Rail that is probably there all winter, though usually invisible.

Sanctuary Pond – pity the birds don't seem to realize it.

OK. So that's the Highgate Ponds done. Where next? Time to turn left (west, I think it is). This takes us across 'The marsh', which is about as official as its name gets. Not that it's a totally appropriate epithet, since all it is a slightly boggy area that looks as if it ought to attract Snipe but never does. It does, however, sport a rather fetching variety of wildflowers and brackeny, reedy stuff that I haven't identified but which provides ideal perches if there are Whinchats or Stonechats around (though neither is common on the Heath).

South Meadow

Then it's on through South Meadow. Another misnomer which harks back to a time when it wasn't overgrown with small oak trees. Peter can remember this area when it was the sort of scrubby habitat beloved of Yellowhammers and Whitethroats, both of which used to breed there. Not any more. To give them their due, the Corporation came up with a plan to clear a lot of the trees. Alas, the Hampstead 'Save our Heath' lobby soon sprang into action and we even had local celebrities threatening to lie down in front of the bulldozers. I volunteered to drive them. Of course, nothing happened; the plan was dropped, and it seems as if South Meadow will never again live up to its name. Nevertheless, it is still a pretty good area, often attracting roving mixed tit flocks, sometimes with attached warblers in the autumn, and with a line of birches and alders worth checking for Siskins and Redpolls in winter.

The Vale Of Health

After South Meadow, there is a choice. We can turn north and check out the Vale of Health. This sheltered dip is so called because it was one of the few places to escape the ravages of the Great Plague of London. You see, local patchwork teaches you a bit of history too. These days most of the Vale is filled with desirable Hampstead residences pretending they are in the country. There is also a small lily pond with more fishermen than birds. The chief interest of the Vale is that it contains one of the very few vestiges of real Heathland, in the form of a small patcn of gorse. It is not very big, but it did entice a singing Dartford Warbler a couple of Mays ago. The excitement at this report was tempered a little by looking up ancient records and discovering that Dartford Warblers actually bred on the Heath at the turn of the century. The birding must have been *really* good back in those days. As well as the gorse, there's a line of large conifers which always have a few Coal Tits in them and usually Goldcrests, and better still, on more than one occasion a singing Firecrest.

Prior's Field

After the Vale of Health (if we've made it that far) it's back south to Prior's Field, or we might have decided to go there in the first place. Or maybe just I did. In fact, I sort of regard Prior's Field as my own special area. It's a little bit out of the way for Peter and Mark, who both live on the other side of the Heath. For me, it's on my way home. There have been quite a few occasions when I've had it to myself, and I have to confess I quite like that. Heaven knows, I don't gloat over gripping off my chums, to use twitcher's parlance ('gripping off' means seeing a good bird which your friends miss and, well, almost taunting them about it. Not nice really). Nevertheless, I think most fellow local patchers would confess that there is a little streak of rivalry amongst them. It is nice to actually find good stuff for yourself. It is also nice to share it. So if I *did* find anything on Prior's Field, I'd be off and running to call back Mark and Peter, or at least I'd ring them as soon as I got home. And what is Prior's Field? Well, it's another of the few bits of the Heath that almost looks heathlike. It's quite a big open slope with a few sandy patches, some long grassy areas, a small damp stream with a patch of stunted reeds, a couple of isolated bramble patches and three or four wooden benches. It can be good for pipits, Wheatears or chats, and I once heard a Nightingale there. On the other hand, it is just as likely to be covered in picnickers and dog-walkers, and to be totally birdless.

Hampstead Ponds

Finally, there are the Hampstead Ponds. Their layout is much the same as in the Highgate valley. There are three of them, in a row, all fairly small. The top one is the Mixed Bathing Pool. There's a fenced-off area, with changing rooms and even a nudist enclosure down one end. The other end is lined with fishermen and voyeurs. There's not much in between, certainly rarely any birds.

Hampstead Two is largely a fishing pond, but there is a raft in the middle, and in some years Mute Swans build a nest amongst half-submerged willows. And last of all, there is Hampstead One (numbering backwards as we're leaving the Heath; it would be the first thing you came to if you were entering from Hampstead Heath Railway Station or the official carpark). There is a notice on this pond that tells you that it is 'Reserved for Wildfowl' and there is a 'No Fishing' sign, where Cormorants like to perch and get an easy laugh. Rather like at Highgate, dogs love to practise their stick-chasing dives here, but the far bank belongs to local houses and is therefore fenced and pretty undisturbed. Grebes and ducks may well lurk under there, and there is an almost permanent Heron stalking the shallows.

So that's it then. That's the usual circuit. In truth, our route covers by no means all of those 792 acres, but you can't do it all and if we tried, that way would madness surely lie. As I said, I think you need to define local patch boundaries and more or less stick within them.

I think of the Heath as *my* place. Or at least *our* place. Sometimes I meet up with Peter and/or Mark. But even if I'm alone it's still a social event. If I'm not talking to my friends, I'm talking to myself! Albeit under my breath. I am constantly thinking, reminiscing, theorizing, anticipating or comparing. What was here last week? Last month, last year, last century even? What do I expect to see? What do I hope to see? We relive past glories and disappointments and we experience new ones. And if the birds don't 'perform', as they say, we get on to other topics. Sport, music, politics. I might even do a little work. I've certainly written songs and chunks of scripts whilst walking on the Heath. To be honest, I sorted out quite a bit of this book out there.

So, patchwork can be creative in all sorts of ways. It can also be incredibly relaxing. Would it be pretentious to suggest that, at best, it can be an almost meditational experience, concentrating the mind to the exclusion of all other distractions? Well, it *can* be. Mind you, it can also be incredibly frustrating. Let's just say it's really good fun. And it might just do you good.

I have taken up a lot of pages setting the scene, as it were. Now I'm going to try to take you through a year's birding on the Heath. Every single visit is recorded in my notebook. The date, the weather, the time I was out there, and the birds I saw. Some entries are quite full, more like a diary. Others are not much more than facts and figures. But, whatever the style, I only have to flick back through the pages to recall and relive any particular day. So here are a dozen accounts of events which I hope will convey to you some of the experience of working a local patch. Most of all, I hope they will make you want to have a go yourself.

1995

During the year I visited the Heath 106 times. The least active periods were February, June and July, with barely one visit per week. The most active were during the migration periods of spring and autumn, with three or four visits per week in April, September and October, and also during continuing hard weather in December. Almost all my visits were early morning, getting out on Parliament Hill as near to dawn as I could manage. Afternoons on the Heath are usually disappointing, probably largely because of the amount of disturbance from people and dogs, but also because migration tends to be more visible in the mornings and the birds are likely to be more active when they are feeding. However,

Below Prior's Field in autumn.
Right Highgate First Pond in winter.

this 'mornings only' rule certainly doesn't apply to all local patches. In fact, evening has always been one of my favourite times and, for example, at reservoirs and gravel pits, very productive birdwise. But the old 'dawn and dusk are best for birds' rule doesn't generally apply on the Heath. At least one advantage of the early morning schedule is that it's worth popping out before going off to work, even if it's only for half an hour or so. Believe me, there are less exhilarating ways of beginning a day than watching the sun rise from the top of Parliament Hill. Mind you, there are less exhausting ways too!

10 FEBRUARY

Wind. South west force 0–1.

A grey, calm morning after a soggy night.

0815 to 1030 hours.

Will winter ever end? Will it ever begin?

I was up on top of Parliament Hill not all that much after dawn, though there was no visible sunrise to mark the occasion. Talking of Mark … he seems to have disappeared. I haven't seen him or even heard from him for several weeks. Presumably he's working abroad. Peter wasn't out this morning either, though I did bump into him a few days ago, the first time we've met up for a while. The only really good bird he's had lately was a Peregrine Falcon, which circled round for a few minutes before heading off back towards the city. Apparently, there have been one or two reported from near the Thames in the middle of London this winter, so it was no doubt one of these. Incredible to think that not that many years ago, you'd have to search the remote crags of Scotland or Wales to find a Peregrine. Maybe they'll even start nesting on skyscrapers like they do in Chicago. Anyway, alas, I had an instant feeling I was *not* going to see one today. To be honest, it didn't feel very 'birdy'.

The weathermen had forecast a cold snap, but it failed to materialize. Instead, it was one of those murky clammy mornings that symbolize that syndrome people are supposed to suffer from in the middle of winter. SAD, is it? Perhaps it stands for Sod All Doing! Birdwise, that is. The problem is this isn't real winter weather. Icy winds, hard frost, snow, I actually enjoy. It certainly gets things going on the Heath. For a start, it looks fantastic dressed in white. And the people look pretty good dressed in woolly hats and coloured scarves. Parliament Hill covered in sledgers and skiers always reminds me of a Bruegel painting. And they don't scare the birds off 'cos if there are any they are usually flying way overhead. Flocks of Lapwings, Skylarks, maybe even Golden Plover, fleeing ahead of the hard weather, off down to the south-west or maybe across to Ireland. I love weather movements, but there haven't been any this year. It has just been too mild.

Mind you, even mild winters are the best time for some local patches. Reservoirs, gravel-pits, estuaries all see more action during the winter months. In fact, wildfowl gather there *because* it's mild. Well, milder than on the Continent where they breed. Plus a bit of unusual weather can always bring something odd in. I remember always racing out to my Birmingham Reservoir if it got foggy or started blowing a gale. A Great Northern Diver wailing in the mist admitting it was lost. A Leach's Petrel skittering over mini white caps pretending it was crossing the Atlantic. Ah, memories! But not today. Probably not ever on the Heath. Let's face it, winter isn't really the most exciting time here. Nevertheless, it is by no means birdless.

Common, Herring, Lesser Black Back and Black-headed Gulls.

OK, there was nothing at all in the skies over the Hill but the playing fields had a nice selection of gulls on them. In fact, a dog-walker commented: 'There's a lot of seagulls today, eh?'

I just smiled and nodded. Of course, I should really have given her a quick lecture.

'There's no such thing as 'seagulls'. As it happens, there are four – or possibly five – different species marching around on that football pitch. Lots of Black-headeds – which don't have black heads because they're in winter plumage – thirty-three Common Gulls – which aren't all that common actually – no fewer than forty-five Herring Gulls, eight Lesser Black Backs – of both British and Scandinavian races – and... an adult Yellow-legged Gull, which some people think is only a Continental race of Herring Gull, but others reckon is a separate species. What's more, it's the first I've ever seen on Hampstead Heath. Impressed?'

Well, her dog obviously was, as it was suddenly seized by an irresistible urge to scatter the whole lot into the air. And quite a dramatic sight they made too.

The hedges were as empty as they usually are in February. Just the 'residents', if I really looked for them, eight Greenfinches, huddled in the hawthorns at the bottom of Second Hedge, with half-a-dozen House Sparrows for company. Maybe that's why the Greenfinches are always there. House Sparrows are notoriously unadventurous. Maybe they found that spot first, and the Greenfinches thought, 'Those sparrows look pretty well fed, we'll latch on to them.' But the Sparrows never go anywhere else. So now, neither do the Greenfinches. Of course, it all makes sense. It's sheltered in there, there must be enough to eat, and they don't waste energy by racing around. Sensible winter survival tactics. And it makes them easy for us birdwatchers to tick them off on the day list.

And what about winter visitors? There are still berries on the hawthorns, but only a single Redwing eating them. Though I checked every alder and birch tree on the circuit, I only found one party of a dozen Siskins. Not a single Redpoll. Those two species really have swapped places. Only five or six years ago there was always a fair-sized winter flock of Redpolls on the Heath, and hardly any Siskins. Now, it's completely the other way around. Apparently it's happening all over the country. What's more, I don't think anyone has come up with any theories as to why this is. This year, though, even the Siskins are in modest numbers. Let's hope we're not going to lose them as well.

Cormorant.

Nothing amazing on the ponds today either. Well, not to a jaundiced old birder like me. In fact, the public seem endlessly amazed by the Cormorants. It's also amazing how people seem to be able to walk past them for weeks and weeks before they suddenly notice them.

'Excuse me, Mr Oddie... I always walk my dog past the ponds. Yesterday, I saw an enormous big black bird perched on the No Fishing sign.'

'It's a Cormorant.'

'Really? Well, I've never seen one of those before!'

Well, Peter can remember a time when Cormorants were pretty rare birds on the Heath, but that was just after World War Two. The fact is there have been masses of Cormorants perched on the signs and rafts or swimming around the ponds for the past five winters at least. Mmm, it makes you think maybe some people just aren't meant to be birdwatchers. I mean, if you can't spot a Cormorant, how are you going to get on with little brown warblers?

Nobody fails to spot the Great Crested Grebes. Today, there were already seven birds back – I presume they go off to bigger reservoirs for the winter – including two pairs displaying to each other and checking out nest sites, including the one that usually moors its platform right by the path on the Boating Pond. I must remember to bring a camera.

Come to think of it, the Grebes weren't the only sign of spring. There was a pair of Sparrowhawks displaying – doing that weird slow-motion tumbling flight – and Missel Thrushes, Nuthatches and Tree Creepers singing heartily – well, as heartily as a Tree Creeper can! And all three species of Woodpecker either calling or drumming. In fact, I had one of the best views I have ever had of a male Lesser Spotted, dangling in a small oak in First Hedge, no more than a couple of yards away, with its little red cap glowing in a ray of winter sunshine. That's the sort of image I'll never forget. Close my eyes any time in the future and I will always be able to 'see' that bird. Nice one.

So, not quite such a SAD day after all. Signs of spring.

Now what I really want is some 'vis mig' – visible migration. Birds flying over on their way south. Please.

Lesser Spotted Woodpecker.

19 MARCH

Wind, north-west force 1–2.

Clear and cool.

0730–0830 hours.

Meadow Pipits aren't meant to be summer visitors but to me they are often the first signs of spring. The fact is that quite a few of our British pipits do go south for the winter, and they fly back up north to breed. This morning three of them flew over me! They weren't even together, so it was hardly a spectacular experience. Each one was just a little dot, fluttering purposefully into the north-west wind, uttering barely audible little 'tseeps'. But audible enough because that was how I picked them up. 'Tseep'… 'Meadow Pipit!' Peter looked bewildered. 'I can't hear them any more,' he muttered, and I couldn't help feeling a little sad for him. For a moment, I reflected how absolutely devastated I shall feel if – or is it when? – my hearing begins to deteriorate. Then a distant noise broke the mood. 'Tseep!' Another one. 'There it is. Just below the Wood Pigeon.' And this time Peter saw it. Even better: it turned back, circled, and called again… and Peter heard it. He was clearly elated. So was I.

Ironical, isn't it? Only a couple of days ago, I was basking in the sun and splashing around in the turquoise waters of the Seychelles, not knowing whether to focus my binoculars on bikini-clad lovelies or on Fairy Terns and Tropic Birds, and now here I am shivering on top of Parliament Hill, getting all worked up at hearing a little brown bird go 'tseep'. And which experience gave me the biggest thrill? 'Tseep'. Am I weird or what?! And 'tseep' again… there goes number three. It's great to be back. I hope the Meadow Pipit was thinking the same thing.

Mind you, it's about the only spring migrant that *is* back. Apparently, about a week ago there was a mild spell that no doubt lured the first Wheatears, Sand Martins and Chiffchaffs to the south coast. Those three are usually the earliest arrivals. But none of them has made it to the Heath yet. All we've got is a single Blackcap, which was singing in a sycamore just behind my house this morning. But had it arrived from the south or had it been lurking around in Hampstead gardens all winter, as more and more Blackcaps have been tending to do in recent years? Probably it thought it had better start singing to establish its territory, just on the off-chance that any of its potential rivals might have flown in from the Continent.

Even if the real summer visitors aren't in yet, as always by mid-March, there is evidence that birds are on the move. While I was away, Peter had a Woodcock and a Short-eared Owl, both once-a-year birds on the Heath – if that – and both no doubt heading back up to the woods or moorlands of northern Britain. Following the pipits in fact. Also, the Redwings are beginning to sound friskier. Today there was a little pack of twenty-five of them posing on a treetop and chortling away. Not quite full song. Just warming up. As indeed the weather is, which is of course what's telling them it's time to get back to Scandinavia. It's about this time that you start hearing them going over at night. Another 'tseeeep' call, but much longer and thinner than pipits'. Non-birders probably think they're bats, if they notice them at all.

The playing fields were almost gullless. Only three Black-headeds, all with black heads this time, so they'll be off any day now too. I remember once going up to the north coast of Scotland at this time of year and being surprised that the Black-headed Gull colony was already in full swing. And it was actually perfectly mild up there. It's the effect of the Gulf Stream I think. Indeed, there were all sorts of birds displaying and mating and nest-building. And yet in mid-winter it would probably have been utterly bleak and birdless. It really makes you realize that it's not just the official migrants that migrate. The fact is there are really very few species of bird that don't change location from winter to summer. Some go only a few hundred yards. Some a few miles. Some from inland to the coast. Others vice versa. Some travel hundreds of miles, some thousands. Some by day, some at night. Some alone, some in flocks. And how do they do it? Oh, they navigate by the stars, or the earth's magnetic

Meadow Pipit cowering from a fighting kite.

force, or maybe echo sounding, or by recognizing landmarks. Call it instinct. Or how about calling it a miracle?

Certainly, if anyone asked me to sum up, in one word, the single most thrilling aspect of birds and bird watching, the word would be: 'migration'.

And what set me off on that little reverie? Oh yes, 'tseep'. Another Meadow Pipit.

OK, but when are we going to get the *real* spring visitors? We need a better breeze.

21 APRIL

Wind, light south-easterly.

0635–1100 hours.

An east wind. This has to be good. The only possible problem is it might be *too* good. The skies are clear after a crisp, almost frosty dawn. Last night must have been perfect for migrants to be on the move. The question is will they think, 'Oh, this is great flying weather,' and just carry on? Or will a few of them drop down on to the Heath? And will we see them?

Such were my thoughts as I arrived on top of the Hill just after half past six. Five minutes later, a Cuckoo answered my question. Cuckoos are not common in Hampstead. This one had clearly felt the need to pause for a rest on its way to somewhere else. It called. Once. Five minutes later, Peter arrived and was a bit miffed to have missed it. As a consolation, a Garden Warbler burst into song from somewhere in the depths of the First Hedge.

Peter and I exchanged notes on the spring migration so far in April. It had been slow and somewhat sporadic. There had been small falls of warblers – Chiffchaffs on the 2nd and 8th, and Willow Warblers on the 3rd – but most of them had moved on through. Blackcaps had certainly increased to the point that we could be confident that they were genuine migrants and not local 'liggers'. Wheatears: so far only a couple of singles. On the 9th, I'd ticked off a Sedge Warbler, no doubt bound for Brent Reservoir, since they never linger here, and a single Swallow – which doesn't make a spring! – along with a lone House Martin. This one was actually very early. The few Martins that breed in the sadly diminishing colonies near the Heath don't usually arrive till the 20-something

of April. So this one was probably carrying on up north.

Redstart.

I'd also had a few odds and ends,
such as a male Gadwall and a couple of Shelduck, both good flyovers for
the Heath. The latter had suddenly appeared, flapping frantically, from
the direction of the Model Boating Pond where they had probably just
been torpedoed! They headed off north-west, and it was no doubt the
same pair that gained permanent fame in the log-book at Brent
Reservoir later in the morning. I've always suspected that the few interesting wildfowl we get on the Heath Ponds have a Brent connection.
This proved it.

Otherwise, winter visitors – Redwings, Fieldfares and a few Siskins and Redpolls – had all been noted moving out in the small numbers we usually get. Now most of them were gone. What's more, the frequent clear skies probably meant that the majority of the incoming migrants had just kept going, high over the Heath, invisible even to our binoculars. Until today. It felt promising, and we resolved to do a thorough full circuit.

We maintained the Parliament Hill vigil for nearly two hours. The Cuckoo never called again, and the Garden Warbler exhausted itself and went quiet. In truth, the sky was hardly alive with vis mig. One Meadow Pipit, five separate Linnets, half-a-dozen Goldfinches and a single Skylark went over. Not a lot, and yet enough to keep us optimistic as we set off along the Second Hedge. Sounds of spring: a Chiffchaff singing its name, then the wispy cascading song of a Willow Warbler, almost drowned out by the fruity burble of a Blackcap. All new in. Then, just as we were cursing a rollicking black Labrador for snuffling into potential bird cover, out flicked one of the birds we were hoping for. A flash of scarlet. A male Redstart. Presumably 'start' is some ancient term for 'tail'. We apologized to the dog for misconstruing its motives as we admired the bird it had so considerately flushed for us. Some birds cock their tails, some flick them. Redstarts tremble theirs. It is a wonderful movement, as if the feathers are vibrating on a spring. This, plus an orange-flushed breast and smoky-black bib qualify male Redstarts as one of our prettiest birds. At the foot of the Third Hedge, we found another. These, along with several more singing Willow Warblers, were sure proof that the east breeze was doing its job.

At ten-thirty I had to leave, as I had work to get back to. I wasn't pleased. Clearly things were happening and, even as I bade farewell to Peter, a Common Tern came screeching over our heads, plunged into the first Highgate Pond and came up with a tiddler in its beak. We wondered if it had noticed the wooden rafts which would surely make perfectly good Tern nesting sites (for the outcome, see my entry for July 13th, page 135). As I set off back over the Hill, I really was convinced – and, to be honest, just a little concerned – that Peter would 'grip me off' after I'd gone. My consolation was Prior's Field, which I would cross on the way home. And it worked. As I hurried across the short grass, three Swallows overtook me on their way north. I paused to admire them, and, since I'd stopped, I took a moment to scan around. I remember thinking that this was about as near to a tiny bit of moorland as we had round here.

A Wheatear obviously agreed with me, as it popped up on to a nearby bench, thus giving us both better views of one another. It obviously wasn't too keen on what it saw, as it then flew to the very top branch of the highest tree on the Field. This is a habit we've noticed before on the Heath. Wheatears are generally thought of as ground-loving birds, but their escape route, if there are trees around, is invariably upwards. What's more, they will stay up there for ages. As I waited to cross the road leaving the Heath, I looked back. I could still see the tiny speck of a bird perched on the top branch, totally motionless, waiting for birdwatchers, dogs and joggers to buzz off so it could drop back down and get on with feeding.

Throughout my working day, I couldn't help but keep glancing out of my office window. The breeze was freshening and the visibility deteriorating. This is what birders refer to as 'blocking' weather. It means that the clear anticyclonic conditions – as last night and this morning – have got the birds on the move, but then a front of poorer weather acts as an invisible wall to their progress. Flying conditions aren't so attractive, and down come the migrants.

I don't usually bother with the Heath in the evenings, but theory and instinct sent me back there. It was pretty murky by the time I got to the sheltered slope at the foot of the Third Hedge. But the gloom was lit up by little pale lights hopping around in the grass: the creamy breasts of Wheatears. First one, then two... no... three... or is it four? It really did seem as though they were dropping from the sky as I watched, and indeed they probably were. They kept popping up and down in the dips, or hopping on to clumps of grass, and the constant activity made it hard to count them. It was almost dark as I scanned for the last time. One... two... five... or was it

How many Wheatears?

Ring Ousel.

six? However many there were, it was nothing compared to what you might see at a coastal location in spring. It wouldn't even be a remarkable number for the banks of many an inland reservoir. Indeed, it certainly wasn't a record count for the Heath. But, believe me, that evening those six Wheatears sent me home very happy indeed.

An hour or two later, I rang Birdline South East. That day, Dungeness and other places in Kent had enjoyed a large fall of migrants. We on the Heath had received the overspill, as it were. It is always nice when the theories are proved right and the connections work out. My only pang of jealousy was news of a Ring Ousel at Brent Reservoir... my old patch. As it turned out, we even put that right two days later when I found not one but two Ring Ousels on the slopes of Parliament Hill. To celebrate the occasion Mark had returned from his travels to enjoy the birds with me. Mmm, yes, it is amazing how he always seems to be there for the good birds!

27 MAY

Late at night.

May is undoubtedly one of my favourite months. Now it's almost over, and I've missed most of it! On the Heath, I mean. I've also missed some pretty good birds. Naturally, Mark saw them. Not that he didn't try and make sure that I did too. Birdwatching is cruel sometimes. As this sad little tale shows, for example.

On May 7th I joined a four-man team from *Birdwatch* magazine to take part in this year's national Bird Race. If you want to know more about bird racing turn to page 169. Meanwhile, suffice it to say that I was up at 2.30 a.m., tazzed round a large chunk of London for nearly twenty-four hours, saw a not terribly impressive ninety-six species, and collapsed into bed a few minutes short of midnight. Not surprisingly, I was not up at dawn the next morning on top of Parliament Hill. But Mark and Peter were, and it was from there that, at about 7 a.m., Mark was frantically trying to call me on his mobile phone. He knew that I would be fast asleep – recovering from the bird race – but he reckoned I wouldn't

Red Kite – *used* to be common in London in the seventeenth century – but *NOT* nowadays.

mind being woken up under the circumstances. Alas, he couldn't get through. My wife Laura works for Talk Radio and that morning she was involved in a *Breakfast Show* broadcast. A phone-in, no less. Using our phone. To be honest, the odds against anyone ringing our house at seven o'clock in the morning and finding our number engaged are pretty astronomical. About as likely as a Red Kite floating over Hampstead Heath in fact. But that is exactly what was happening.

Mark spotted the bird soaring in from the west. Then it stopped, and began circling. It was still half a mile or so from the top of the Hill. It was, in fact, over South End Green, where I live. Mark was desperately trying to call me to say that there was a once-in-a-lifetime bird hovering right over my house. To see it, all I would have had to do was roll over in bed and look out of the window! Of course, by the time Laura's broadcast was over, the Kite was long gone. At least Mark was kind enough to let me carry on snoozing and break the news gently to me later in the day. Naturally I was generous enough to be very happy for Mark and Peter. I was also very sorry for myself!

But we must look on the bright side. Our Bird Race tally hadn't been very impressive. The weather had been clear, warm and westerly, and consequently there had been very few of those late winterers or passing migrants that can boost the total. Nevertheless, we had got a very good impression of the current status of many of London's birds. The abundance of one particular species was special cause for satisfaction. There were Whitethroats everywhere. Not only were they singing from the sort of brambly patches you'd expect, we even came across birds in the oddest of places. Down by Docklands, or in the garden of an East End pub. I like Whitethroats. Not only are they perky little birds to look at, but they are considerate enough to deliver their scratchy little songs from conspicuous perches or – better still – during their cascading display flight. This sometimes makes them very easy to see (always a virtue in a bird, I reckon). Mind you, at other times they can be devilishly skulking, but even that is rather fun, 'cos it's always a challenge to 'dig one out', and they can get your adrenalin going by making you think they might be something rarer, before they finally pop out and give themselves up. All in all, good-value birds. I remember them being very common in the Midlands countryside when I was a lad. I also recall being saddened and then dismayed when their population crashed during the seventies. The theory was that thousands, probably millions, of birds were starving to death on their wintering grounds, due to severe droughts in the African Sahel. For almost a couple of decades the British countryside was largely deprived of the Whitethroat's cheery chattering. But in recent years they seem to be making a comeback; 1995 was a very good year. On race day, we

Whitethroat.

found them all over London. Throughout May, several sang or skulked about on the Heath.

Oriole.

With the Whitethroats came the other species typical of the second wave of spring migrants. Dutifully we noted the arrival dates and compared them with previous years. Two Lesser Whitethroats and a Whinchat in the Hedges on the 3rd. Reed Warblers back singing in the Sanctuary Pond reed-bed on the 6th. Bang on schedule. Swifts circling over my house a couple of days later, announcing their arrival as usual by screaming their heads off. Or were they still panicking after seeing a Red Kite?

By mid-month, Swift numbers were up to our local breeding population and I saw birds swooping under the eaves, checking out nesting sites. Meanwhile, the Hampstead House Martins were gathering mud for their nests, but the colonies are still woefully small compared with, say, ten years ago. On the 17th, another Cuckoo called and moved on; a Yellow Wagtail flew over, calling loudly as if asking the way to somewhere marshier; and I saw the first Spotted Flycatcher of the year. It was obviously a new arrival, looking a bit bemused on a lone tree on the middle of Prior's Field, which is definitely not prime flycatcher habitat. No doubt within a day or two it would have discovered some nice ivy-covered ruin where it would feel sufficiently at home to settle down to nest. Come to think of it, the Spotted Flycatcher is one of the very few late migrants that do breed on the Heath these days. It's all to do with loss of habitat of course, usually in the name of 'tidying up'. Peter can recall the days gone by when there were much larger patches of bramble and scrub, and consequently far more nest sites for the warblers that need that sort of cover. Unfortunately, much of the management in the past paid heed to those of the public who like their open spaces more park-like. The current regime – the Corporation – is more inclined to 'let things go' a bit, which will suit the wildlife, but I fear it's probably too late.

Nevertheless, migrants pass through the Heath in May, just as they do any local patch. Of course the peak times vary with geography. To put it simply, spring is later the further north you go. And of course vice versa. Species like Chiffchaffs and Willow Warblers, could be feeding young by mid-May near the south coast, whilst they are still arriving on their breeding haunts up in the Northern Isles. Consequently, for the migrant-hungry birdwatcher, it makes sense to travel north with the spring.

This is exactly what I often try to do. In mid-May 1995 I went as far north as I could go in Britain, to the very top of Shetland. I had been invited to open a splendid new Information Centre at the even more splendid seabird colony at Hermaness. Having gone that far, I persuaded myself that I might as well stay on for a week and enjoy the Shetland spring. Except, alas, it didn't seem to have arrived yet. I spent several days tramping around in snow-storms in search of migrants. Not surprisingly I didn't find very many, although a few did manage to struggle through. My most enduring memory is of leaning on a garden wall and realizing I was sharing my shelter with a handsome male Golden Oriole, which was sitting on a log, all fluffed up against the cold, no doubt wondering how on earth it had ended up in Shetland instead of Spain. Or indeed Suffolk or Norfolk. Or, for that matter, Hampstead Heath.

Yes, such is the irony of birding that when I got back to London and called Mark to find out what I'd missed while I'd been away, he told me that the best bird had been – you guessed it – a male Golden Oriole.

May is definitely a 'rare bird month'. Which brings me to today, the 27th. I didn't go on the Heath. I stayed in working and then went out to a jazz club for the evening. By the time we got back it was nearly mid-night. I was just about to open the front door when I heard a familiar bird call coming from somewhere up above me. For a second I almost ignored it. I had heard the same sound often enough a few days before up in Shetland. Then I remembered I was now back in Hampstead. 'Peeep. Peeep,' it called again. Clearly and unmistakably, it was an Oystercatcher. It was pitch-dark and I couldn't see it, but it was certainly making sure I heard it. Maybe it was trying to tell me something: 'Hey, listen, I know I'm not a Red Kite, but in my way I'm just as rare. I mean, when did anyone last record an Oystercatcher on Hampstead Heath? I'll tell you when… never, that's when.'

Mmm. Midnight. I suppose it's too late to phone Mark. But next morning I did. He was suitably impressed.

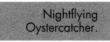

Nightflying Oystercatcher.

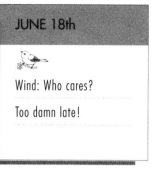

JUNE 18th

Wind: Who cares?

Too damn late!

A day I'd like to forget, but never will…

The Little Bittern is rather a splendid bird. It is, as the name implies, smaller than the common Bittern. A lot smaller. Hardly bigger than a Moorhen really. This makes it very hard to see, especially since it spends most of its time hidden deep in reed-beds. This is a pity, since it's quite a pretty bird, with a little black cap and lovely creamy wing patches. I've seen quite a few Little Bitterns in Spain and Cyprus. But never in Britain. Little Bittern is a very rare bird here. The sort of bird one dreams of seeing on your local patch. Now read on…

It was Sunday, June 18th. I wasn't in a very good mood anyway. In the afternoon, I hadn't much enjoyed watching Jonah Lomu trampling all over the England Rugby team in the semi-final of the Rugby World Cup. What's more, it was Father's Day, which for some perverse reason always slightly depresses me. My wife and daughters had taken me out for an evening meal, but I confess I had been ungraciously dull company. However, if I was morose when I got back home, I was soon to become almost suicidal. The light on my answering machine was blinking three times. The first message was from Mark.

'Bill, I've just had a call from some bloke who says there's a Night Heron on the Leg of Mutton Pond on West Heath. I'm off up there now.'

Well, that must have been about eight o' clock I reckoned. It was now half past ten, and dark. No point in going. In fact I wasn't all that upset. A Night Heron is a pretty rare bird but it's easy enough to convince yourself that one found in London in the middle of June has possibly escaped from some cage or other. In any case, I've seen a couple in the UK that had much better credentials. So I merely sighed, and played the second message. It was Mark again, now on his mobile.

'I'm at Leg of Mutton. I'm looking at the bird. It's not a Night Heron. It's much better. It's a female Little Bittern!'

Now I felt sick. I played the third message. It was Dick Filby from the Rare Bird Alert Pager service.

'Bill, do you realize there's a Little Bittern on Hampstead Heath?'

Yup. Thanks, Dick. (Actually, I haven't, even now, got round to thanking him for the call. I do hope he's reading this, so he'll know why.) What a great Father's Day present, eh? A Little Bittern, which would have been a British tick for me, less than a mile from my house. I'd gone out half

Little Bittern.

an hour before the first call, and had got back half an hour after the last one. Now it was pitch-dark.

I didn't sleep that night. Monday morning, before 4 a.m., I was standing by the Leg of Mutton Pond. So were several other birders, and indeed – within the hour – so was Mark, bless him. He cut a splendidly incongruous figure in his City suit. Typical of him not merely to have ticked off the bird the previous evening, but to have come out again to share the experience and marshal the twitch at dawn the next day. But alas, it was not to be. We all agreed that the Little B. *should* have still been there. It had been found 'by accident' at a place way off our normal circuit by a bloke who just happened to be doing some kind of nature survey in the area. Surely it had been present for days, or even weeks. So why should it go? But it did. It was never seen again.

I still think about that incident and get a nasty twist in the tummy. But it did have some consolations. Not least, the camaraderie amongst fellow 'dippers'. Also, there was, as Mark put it, a Pythonesque element to the twitch. Not only was the bird initially misidentified, but so was the pond. The first bulletin on Birdline went out as 'Night Heron at Bushy Park', which is where the more famous Leg of Mutton Pond happens to be. (The one that has at least had more than a Moorhen on it in the past, unlike the grotty little puddle on the far side of the Heath where we normally never go.) The message was eventually corrected, but whether some birders actually missed the Hampstead Bittern by going to look for the Bushy Park Heron, I don't know. (If they did, I fear they shouldn't expect much sympathy from me!) So that was pretty farcical.

However, what added the truly exquisitely surreal touch was that the Leg of Mutton Pond just happens to be situated bang slap in the middle of Hampstead Heath's traditional gay 'trawling' area. Frankly, it's famous for it. What's more, Sunday night is – how shall I put it?? – a time of peak activity. Heaven knows, they're probably used to the odd peeping Tom, but how did they react to fifty rough-hewn lads with binoculars, done up in a variety of paramiliatry costumes that would have upstaged the Village People? They must have thought they'd been invaded by a voyeurs' convention! In any event, be honest, it added a certain something to the dawn dip-out. I shall never forget the moment a blushing birder came stumbling out of the bushes shrieking that he'd just been confronted by a naked man with the greeting: 'Ooh! Is that a telescope in your pocket, or are you just pleased to see me?'

A case of 'Once Bittern – twice shy'? And they say June is one of the dullest months on a local patch!

13 JULY

Wind, south-south-east force 2.

Clearing up after overnight rain. 0815–1000 hours.

Technically, it is bang slap in the middle of summer, but in the bird world the autumn has begun.

I often think July is an underrated month. It is definitely at this time that return migration gets underway. Particularly for waders. I'm willing to bet that if I took a trip to some coastal mudflats – down in Kent for example – I'd find there were little parties of adult birds – Dunlin, Knot, maybe even Curlew Sandpipers or Ruffs – that have finished breeding up in the Arctic or in Scandinavia and are already on their way back south. Alas, I have too much work on for even a day trip, so have to stick to the Heath. Not the greatest wader habitat in the world, but it *can* happen. A couple of years ago Peter saw a splendid string of a dozen or more Curlew flapping purposefully south-west. Not a chance of them landing, of course. That's the way you see waders at inland sites. Flying over. With any luck, they'll call and draw attention to themselves, but you can't bank on it. In fact, the rule often seems to be that single birds tend to be noisy – probably because they're feeling desperately lonely and are frantically trying to make contact with fellow travellers – whilst migrating flocks are often silent – probably because they're confident in their own company. Another rule, that seems to apply to the Heath at least, is that you stand the best chance of spotting migrating waders on grey, even drizzly days. No doubt this is because the weather forces them to fly lower down. Which of course implies that there might well be a lot more waders up there than we realize. We don't see them because they fly too high.

Which brings me to today. There was some rain last night, which I was quite glad about because it

Curlews – not that I saw them.

meant I wasn't tempted to get out at first light. After a bit of a lie-in, I was on the Hill by just after eight o'clock, by which time the sky was almost clear blue. Definitely *not* wader weather. No little birds flying either, but I wouldn't really expect it yet. Instead, I headed almost immediately for the Third Hedge. There has been an enormous tit flock building up in there over the past week. Today, it was truly impressive. The trees were absolutely alive. Over a hundred birds, all fluttering and twittering together. Blue, Great, Long-tailed and Coal Tits, with a few attendant Nuthatches and Tree Creepers. Adults and juveniles. All enjoying one another's company and leading each other to food. No doubt there are masses of insects on, under and around the leaves all along the hedge.

I've been keeping an eye on this flock, waiting for the first warblers of the autumn to latch on to it. Today I found them. There were two Chiffchaffs, both adults, halfway through their moult. They looked really odd. The head and body still had old feathers, now very worn and grey. In contrast, the wings were in nice fresh plumage, with brand-new feathers, quite bright green. Of course, every feather tells a tale as it were. It's an intriguing process. During the time the adults are frantically feeding the young in the nest, their feathers get increasingly bent and battered and by the time the family has fledged, the parents often look a right old mess. They then hide away, deep in the foliage where they can safely lose their worn-out old wing feathers. During this time they probably can't fly so well, so they would be vulnerable to predators – hence the hiding.

They can't feed so efficiently either, so they no doubt get hungry too. Then, when their wings are back in action, out they come. This is when they can start feeding again

Common Tern.

Chiffchaff.

now, whilst at the same time carrying on the head and body moult. And in hardly a week or so, having grown fresh feathers and taken on fuel, they will be ready to set off on the first part of that arduous and long journey south, perhaps eventually ending up as far down as Africa. Pretty amazing, isn't it?

Meanwhile, those two Chiffchaffs didn't look much like the picture in the field guides.

In fact if I wasn't on Hampstead Heath in the middle of July, I would have been considering various other – rarer – warblers. But they were just Chiffchaffs. And very welcome too.

Even more welcome were a couple of Whitethroats. This is really good news. One adult and a very smart juvenile. There were lots around in spring; now let's hope there are plenty of youngsters in the autumn.

And talking of breeding success… a pair of Common Terns have nested on one of the rafts on the first Highgate Pond, as we'd hoped they would after our sighting on April 21st. Once again, the local patch confirms the national trend. More and more Common Terns seem to be setting up colonies inland these days. I remember, only a few years ago, when they first started occupying the rafts at Brent Reservoir. They were so successful that the Brent Conservation Team had to add more rafts. Then more terns filled them up. This year, I presume they put up a No Vacancies notice at Brent, and so a late pair decided to try the Heath. They have provided fantastic sights and sounds throughout the summer. Displaying, diving for fish and presenting them to one another, and dive-bombing dogs who dared to paddle in 'their' territory. All within a mile or two of the centre of London. By mid-June they were obviously incubating eggs. Then, in early July, we spotted two fluffy little chicks. Unfortunately, so did the Crows. Heaven knows, the Terns have been giving them a hard time, but I reckon the black marauders work in teams. The 'distractors' keep flapping around, lunging and croaking, till both Tern parents are lured away from the raft to chase them off. At which point, in goes the 'snatcher' to try to grab the chick. They've probably been trying this technique for a week or so now. Today, it looks like they've succeeded. We can only see one baby. With any luck, though, this one will survive. It's pretty big and, since it's now an only child, it will no doubt get double protection. All in all, I'm pretty confident that we'll soon be able to say that in 1995 Common Terns bred on Hampstead Heath, as far as I know, for the first time ever.

29 AUGUST

Wind, north-west force 2.

Becoming drizzly.

0645–1050 hours.

August – another month I've largely missed. Laura and I were determined to have a proper long summer holiday for the first time in a few years. Rosie (our nine-year-old daughter) approved of our choice of destination. We were going to spend two weeks on Cape Cod, sharing a chalet in the woods with family friends, followed by a week in Disney World. We had a great time, but there is a little touch of irony in that England has enjoyed its hottest heatwave for years, whilst in Florida it poured down every day! Nevertheless, this I can take, as long as Mark or Peter hasn't 'gripped me off' with a mega rarity on the Heath.

I confess I was just a smidgeon nervous when we met up on the Hill this morning. In fact, it seems I have missed a good month, but nothing that really hurts. The best bird was a Honey Buzzard. This came to them courtesy of the Brent hotline. The regular Reservoir watchers are now armed with mobile phones, as of course is Mark. If any of them sees a good bird that appears to be heading in their direction, they call one another so they can keep a special look-out. Thus, one sunny morning, a Honey Buzzard was seen circling over the reservoir and then heading off south-east. Mark received the call: 'Honey Buzzard heading your way.' The Heath is only a couple of miles from Brent as the Buzzard flies, and, sure enough, a quarter of an hour later Mark spotted it circling over Hampstead. It was no doubt following the recommendation of its very good friend the Red Kite, who'd passed this way earlier in the year. This time I was not asleep in my own bedroom next to an engaged phone. I was at a drive-in movie on Cape Cod. Somehow the distance made the report much more acceptable. I almost surprised myself by being genuinely pleased for my fellow patch-watchers.

Otherwise, Mark and Peter informed me that there had been a constant passage of common migrants on the Heath, and particularly in the Hedges. These had included occasional Wheatears, Whinchats

and Pied Flycatchers, and Heath rarities such as the Wood Warbler, Nightingale and even a Green Sandpiper that had risked land-

Young even-more-spotted Flycatcher

ing in the corner of one of the Highgate Ponds for a few minutes before no doubt panicking away, calling frantically and generally announcing its presence as Green Sandpipers so considerately always do. Why can't all birds be so cooperatively noisy?

A quick circuit today confirmed a reasonable autumn collection and signs of successful local breeding. There were at least two families of Spotted Flycatchers, with the youngsters looking even more spotted than their parents, and at least thirty Willow Warblers and Chiffchaffs mixed in with the roving tit flocks. These warblers, by the way, we tend to refer to simply as 'phylloscs' – the scientific name for their group being 'phylloscopus' – not bothering to distinguish between the two very similar species. A lot of birders do this, though some prefer 'Willow-chiff' as the all-purpose name. The truth is, you *can* tell the difference – though it isn't easy when they're not singing – but since at this time of the migration they seem about evenly mixed, it's hardly worth bother-ing. Later in the year, we try to sort them out, if only to record the last departure dates of each species. Anyway, today there were plenty of both, mainly youngsters. Many of the adults will be a lot further south already. There were also a couple of smart Lesser Whitethroats and –

continuing confirmation of a good year – with no fewer than four Whitethroats. This might not seem a lot to some local patchers, especially those near a coastal migration point which gets hundreds some mornings, but the fact is that some Augusts we've been pushed to find more than a couple on the Heath all month. Four in a day is very good news.

The only sour note is that our Mute Swans have yet again fallen foul of discarded fishing line. Apparently the Swan Rescue Team has been called in several times, and currently we are down to a single adult and a lone cygnet. Hopefully some of those taken away to have hooks or line removed will survive the operation and eventually be returned, but meanwhile, and not surprisingly, a lot of anti-fishing feeling has been expressed. It may be self preservation – bordering on cowardice? – but I don't think I'm going to join in the debate. One of the plusses of being a TV personality (or whatever I am) is that I sometimes can exert a bit of pressure. One of the penalties is that I then become a target of aggression from those who disagree. I am certainly distressed by what happens to the swans, and I'm angry at the thoughtless anglers but, at the same time, I have sympathy for those who have been fishing responsibly on the Heath for generations. I think I'll leave this one to the locals. But then I am a local. Mmm… maybe I should get involved.

Swans: the two that survived.

Meanwhile, back to birding.

2 SEPTEMBER

Wind, north-west force 0–1.

Grey, becoming drizzly.

0630–1215 hours.

One of those really good days.

I met up with Mark and Peter at the crack of what was a rather odd murky dawn. The air was almost dead calm, and it felt like there might be a threat of thunder. To be honest, it wasn't a particularly promising start. Visible migration was limited to fifty House Martins and ten Swallows, though the latter were accompanied by three Sand Martins, which are never common birds here. Then at 7.30 the first 'good bird' dashed purposefully past us: a streamlined, jet-propelled Hobby, racing south as fast as it could. These lovely little falcons have become more frequent on the Heath – and elsewhere – in the London area – in the past few years. Yet another raptor that seems to be making a comeback, no doubt as the result of less poisoning and persecution.

So, was the Hobby a sign that things were 'on the move'? The bottom of the First Hedge seemed to suggest that indeed they were. Or rather, that they probably had been overnight. But if migrants had been moving, it was likely that the deteriorating weather would now be dampening their progress. The evidence was skulking in the bushes before us. First, a Whitethroat popped its head out, then a Garden Warbler, then two Blackcaps and finally two Lesser Whitethroats. All of them were threading their way through a bramble patch within a few feet of each other. All of them were silent, looking almost

Whitethroat, Blackcap and Lesser Whitethroat – instant comparison.

subdued, as if the weather had 'brought them down' both literally and in spirit. In contrast, *our* spirits were rising. The day was beginning to feel very birdy.

The Second Hedge produced more Lesser Whitethroats, and a Whinchat suddenly popped up on a bare branch and disappeared again almost in the same movement. It really was as if the birds were challenging us to dig them out. We continued to do so, despite the fact that increasingly frequent rain showers kept interrupting our search. By midmorning, we found ourselves huddling for shelter under an oak tree in South Meadow, adding up the totals in rather soggy notebooks. Ten Blackcaps, three Whitethroats, four Garden Warblers and at least a dozen Lesser Whitethroats. Plus, a couple of odd 'flyovers': four Snipe and a juvenile Common Gull. Both are species that nest far away from Hampstead. Maybe near the coast. Maybe on real heathland. Perhaps this would be a clue to where 'the big one' might come from. 'The big one' is the rarity that you just hope and pray you are going to find on a day that feels good. Shortly after 11.30 a.m., the big one appeared.

We were trudging back towards the Third Hedge with decidedly mixed feelings. We were elated that there were birds around but dejected that the weather was getting so bad that it was becoming almost impossible to carry on birding. We were also convinced that there should be something really good involved in the movement, but that we might well miss it if we gave up. As it turned out, it was fortuitous indeed that we resolved to give it just a little bit longer, as we headed for the natural umbrella of the Hedge's thickest tree.

I was the first to spot the bird. My glasses were spattered with rain, but I could see enough to know instantly that it was something special. Mind you, I instinctively responded by playing it safe. It was some way off yet, approaching from the west, through the murk. It was clearly quite big, and long-winged. My first – silent – thought was that it could be a large gull. But I knew it wasn't. I called Mark's attention to the bird with a question to which I already partially knew the answer: 'What is *this*?' I asked, confident that it was, in fact, a Harrier. But which one? The truth is, you could probably count the number of Harriers – of any species – that have been recorded over Hampstead Heath on the fingers of one mittened hand, but we still had to take the 'likelihood' approach. This is always the sensible thing to do when confronted by what you suspect – nay, hope – may be a rare bird. Firstly, assume it is a common

Montagu's Harrier.

one. Then, at least, consider the least rare option. This was what Mark did next. 'Is it a Marsh?' he asked. I suspect he too knew he was wrong. What's more, he was probably glad he was. So was I. The next words we spoke were almost immediate, and almost in unison. 'It's a Monty's.'

Indeed it was. The fact that up to now Peter had remained silent was no doubt because he may well not have seen Montagu's Harrier for many many years. Fortunately, both Mark and I were familiar with the species and were able to tick off the identification points as it flew right over our heads and even paused to do a couple of circles before carrying on. The fact that the light was so poor made plumage detail difficult to see, but actually drew attention to the feel and shape of the bird: the 'jizz', as birders call it (see page 32). Slim-bodied, almost falcon-like wings, long tail, a lot of visible head. All quintessential Monty's characteristics, compared with the more robust Hen Harrier or the even sturdier, more Kite-like Marsh. At one point it tipped over and flashed its white rump – the 'ringtail' which is the expression often used to refer to female or juvenile Harriers – and the cinnamon underparts, which suggested that this one was probably a youngster.

Eventually 'the big one' flapped off into the gloom over Highgate Hill. Where had it come from? It flew in from the west. Well, that's odd for a start. The very few pairs we have in Britain breed in the south or east! Maybe it wasn't British at all. Which is odder still, since there's not much land to the west of Britain! The wind had been northerly for several days, so maybe a Scandinavian origin was more likely. Possibly the Snipe and that Common Gull came from there too, not that either called with a Swedish accent. Sometimes the weather's influence on bird movements seems logical, sometimes it doesn't. Or maybe it is, but we just don't understand it. One thing was for certain, that bird had got itself disorientated and was rapidly trying to get back in the right direction. And at least we knew where it was going. Away. Leaving the country, that's for sure. Off to pleasanter climes, and who could blame it on a morning like that?

We did the same. Soaked but happy, as they say, three local patchers returned home to dry out. Mind you, two of us were tempted out again in the afternoon, when the rain had stopped, and Mark and I added Wood Warbler and Pied Flycatcher to the day's list.

The final comment in my notebook said it all. 'Despite the weather – or possibly because of it? – it was a fine day.'

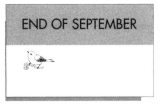

END OF SEPTEMBER

The changing skies

Throughout the month I have spent many a morning on top of Parliament Hill, and most entertaining it has been too. It really is fascinating to witness how the patterns of migration change as the autumn goes by. This year, the contrasts and phases have been particularly vivid.

Early in the month, it is migrants in the Hedges. Then the warblers become less frequent and the Hedges empty, but the sky begins to get busy. First, there is just the occasional Swallow or House Martin gliding south. Then, some years – this one, for example – it becomes a deluge. On several days this September there were hundreds of them. If the breeze was strong they would fly low, always into it, the Swallows skimming the surface of the grass, barely at knee level. Even on calmer days, the Swallows fly lower than the House Martins. The two species definitely have different styles. The Swallows are usually low and direct, whilst the Martins travel higher and are more prone to swirling. This makes them harder to count, as you are never quite sure if you are seeing the same birds circling round, or several separate flocks. I suspect the latter. It is a pretty safe rule that when there are lots of birds – whether they are in the air or in trees – birdwatchers, including me, tend to

underestimate the numbers. There have been days lately when, if you scanned across the sky, you would

Swallows and House Martins.

see maybe 200–300 Swallows and Martins. But this went on all morning, and the sky was never empty, and the truth is that probably nearer 2000 or 3000 passed through during that time. Well, there were certainly an awful lot of birds, which hopefully indicates that there has been good breeding success. I confess I find it immensely exhilarating standing up on the Hill with these birds dashing past me, knowing that over the next few weeks they will also be skimming over the waves of the English Channel, then over the Mediterranean, and possibly the sands of the Sahara, before they finally get to Africa. Surely you don't need to be a birdwatcher to be excited by a phenomenon like that?

However, you probably *do* have to be a birdwatcher to get turned on by most of the other migrants that pass over the Hill. Heaven knows, I can imagine that the dog-walkers and joggers think we must be totally nuts, spending hour after hour gazing almost vertically upwards at apparently invisible birds. Even if we try to show them what we're watching, it's hardly thrilling.

'That little dot is a Yellow Wagtail.'

'Those specks are Linnets.'

We don't even see some of the birds.

'That was a Tree Pipit just called.'

'Can you see it?'

'No. But it definitely is.'

'How do you know?'

'Well… experience.'

I'm afraid that's the only reply I can give.

Identifying bird calls isn't easy. Not bird song, mind you, just calls. Barely audible little 'tsips', 'chups', 'fsweeps' and so on. That's the way they write them in the field guide, but it doesn't really help that much. (Stephen gives some useful guidelines on learning bird songs and calls, and distinguishing between them, on page 31.) All you can do is practise. Over the years, you get to know which birds make what noises. At first, you need a decent view to be sure that you've matched them up correctly. Then you get more confident, even if the bird is some way away, or flying overhead. Eventually you start 'calling them' without seeing the bird at all. Non-birders have no idea how you're doing it, beginners are impressed and ask what the secret is. Like I said, the secret is experience. Believe me, it's worth acquiring, because it really is good fun.

This September, the skies have been full of noises. We have noted a healthy passage of Pipits, mainly Meadows ('tseep'), but also a few Trees ('teeze'), along with Yellow Wagtails ('fsweep') and quite a few Greys ('tzik') and Pieds ('tsizzic'). As with so many birds on the Heath, the numbers weren't huge, but each one was satisfying, testing our skills and reminding us of the miracle of migration.

Then, towards the end of the month, the seed-eaters seemed to take over the airways. On September 20th, we noted half-a-dozen Linnets flying south. Over the following days and into early October, the passage continued and got stronger and stronger, often involving flocks of twenty or thirty birds, and peaking on October 8th with a morning total

Linnet, wondering whether it should join its friends.

of well over 100. Such numbers are, as far as I know, totally unprecedented on the Heath. Another unassuming little brown bird making local headlines! So why so many Linnets? Have they too had a good breeding season, or are these birds travelling on a slightly different route because of an unusual weather pattern? Every year a new puzzle.

Talking of puzzles... the Linnets and other finches seem to conform to this 'single birds make a noise and flocks are often silent' rule. This sets yet another challenge for the migration watcher. Generally we've got maybe four or five species up there: Linnet, Chaffinch, Greenfinch, Goldfinch and possibly Siskin. Any of them are easy enough to identify by call. But if they *don't* call and they are flying in compact little flocks, at considerable speed, some way in the distance, and their characteristic little flashes of colour aren't being caught by the sun... how do you sort them out then? You've guessed it: experience. You get to know the slightly more leisurely flight of the Chaffinches, the slightly stockier build of the Greenfinches, the slightly more bouncy style of the Linnets, and so on... but – I'll own up – there were still a few faraway groups that went down as just 'finches'. No birder can identify everything he or she sees. Accept it. Don't worry. Enjoy.

It has been an enjoyable month.

22 OCTOBER

Wind, west force 0–1.

0620– 0845 hours.

And after the pipits and the wagtails and the finches come the thrushes.

Or at least they should have done. This year it really hasn't happened. The news has been the same from the coast: continuing westerly winds and no winter thrushes. Has there ever been an October when there wasn't a large visible immigration of Redwings and Fieldfares from the Continent? Sometimes it is as early as maybe the 6th or 7th, more often it's around the 14th or 15th. But this year we got past the 20th before anything happened at all. Even then, I don't think it has exactly been a major invasion.

Yesterday, I was in central Kent, opening a garden centre. There was an east wind – usually the signal to release the thrushes – but it was also a crystal-clear day with hardly a cloud in the sky. In fact, I did notice quite

The winter thrushes – three Fieldfares and a Redwing (*right*). Actually the Redwings are usually the commoner of the two.

a few packs of Redwings high overhead, but I suspect that the weather was so good that they probably passed over the coast completely unnoticed. Certainly, when I rang Birdline South East, there were ño great numbers reported from either the Bird Observatories at Dungeness or Sandwich Bay. Nevertheless, I figured there might be a continuing passage over the Heath this morning.

And so it proved to be. I was out at the unearthly hour of 6.20. The clocks went back last night, so it was really 7.20, but this was no consolation at all. The wind had lost its easterly component and dropped to virtually nothing. The sky was still cloudless, though not yet light, which was frustrating, because there were definitely birds up there. I could hear them. First, the thin squeaks of Redwings, and then the hoarse wheeze of Bramblings. These northern cousins of the Chaffinch look more or less identical if they are flying overhead, when you can't see their characteristic white rumps. Fortunately they call completely differently. *Un*fortunately there were Chaffinches up there too; and as the sun rose higher, so did the birds. For over two hours I stayed listening and

counting, but it got more and more frustrating. The birds just got higher and higher and higher. It was quite

Wood Pigeons.

exciting in a way. My ears would pick up a faint call, I'd squint upwards and my eyes would just about spot tiny dots flying over at a very great height. It was a fair bet that I was missing more migration going on way up there beyond human eyesight. The birds I managed to identify comprised quite a mixed bag. As well as the Bramblings and Chaffinches, there were also rather surprising travellers like five Bullfinches and six high-flying Dunnocks. And there were indeed some winter thrushes: only about twenty Fieldfares, but a fair number of Redwings, including one flock of 400, which was quite an impressive sight.

But if it was big numbers and a little mystery I craved, I had to think back to just after first light. First, the big numbers. Throughout the autumn there is a dawn movement of Wood Pigeons over the Heath. Within a few minutes of the sun rising, hundreds of birds appear almost magically out of the gloom and cascade over Parliament Hill – and most of Hampstead and Highgate on either side – heading south. The birds have presumably roosted in various woodlands in North London, and are spreading out over the City parks to feed. They probably straggle back sporadically during the day, as there never seems to be a very obvious return movement. But the morning flight is truly spectacular. Never more so than this morning, when at least 5000 streamed over in less than twenty minutes. Wood pigeons are common enough birds, yes, even considered a nuisance by some, but in such numbers they're really quite thrilling.

And what of the little mystery? Oh yes, I'd been trying to forget that. Even as I arrived on top of the Hill, when it was barely light, in amongst the squeaking of Redwings and the wheezing of Bramblings and the clapping of Pigeon wings…

Snow Bunting.

I heard a single brief snatch of a tinkly call that was almost certainly, but not quite, acceptably, countably, definitely, a Snow Bunting. I had no chance of seeing it in that light, but if it had called just once more I would have been sure of it. How? Experience, of course. Which also tells me the incident is best forgotten. One that got away.

NOVEMBER

A whole month best forgotten.

Not that I had much to remember. I spent most of it out of the country, either touring round Britain with the RSPB's 'Bird in the Nest' roadshow, or filming a 'pilot' programme for a possible birdwatching series in America. It seems I haven't missed much on the Heath. Mark has gone missing again, whilst even Peter seems to have been dispirited enough by lack of birds to have been out only rarely.

Woodlark – but no woods.

He did have one 'goody' on November 7th: a Woodlark, which apparently scuttled from under the cover by the Second Hedge and risked waddling some way towards Parliament Hill before a pack of poodles and a Chinese fighting kite persuaded it that there were more peaceful places to land. It was last seen heading south. Fanciful to imagine, I suppose, that it was the same one that was recorded at Dungeness later that day. At the very least, though, the report on Birdline confirmed that Woodlarks were on the move at the time. Well, at least two of them were.

Otherwise, the year seems to have already come full circle. We're back to basics. Migration has ceased, and the 'resident' population is much the same as it was back in February. The winter doldrums, you could call it. Except that, yet again, it isn't real winter. It is mild, damp and relatively birdless. It won't change unless we get some hard weather.

5 DECEMBER

Wind, east-north-east force 4.

0800–1140 hours.

Hard weather indeed! The birds sense it is on the way. And so do I. Yesterday, I watched the weather forecast: 'An anticyclone over Scandinavia, north-east winds, snow predicted.'

This morning, I was out not long after first light, which is mercifully late these days. In fact my initial circuit was unimpressive and, by just before ten o'clock, I was on my way home. Indeed, I was waiting for a gap in the traffic to allow me to get back into South End Green when I almost absentmindedly looked up. There above me was a high-flying flock of Lapwings heading south-west. It was the sign I'd hoped for, and indeed anticipated.

Lapwings always seem to be the first to flee in front of approaching cold. They are very attractive birds at the best of times, possibly rather taken for granted because they are relatively common. I have always felt, though, that if they were rarer, twitchers would travel miles and mass in hundreds to gasp and drool over them. 'Oh! Brilliant plumage. Look at that green and purple sheen when the sun catches it. Oh and that crest. Oh yeah! Mega gripper that one.' What's more, not only is a single Lapwing a little cracker, they also give rather good value in flocks. I always get a thrill when I am travelling by train in winter and we pass a ploughed field studded with Lapwings. It's even better when a passing raptor, maybe a Merlin, puts them all up, and suddenly the sky is filled by a twinkling cloud of black-and-white. And that's another good thing about Lapwings. Their flight pattern and jizz is so distinctive you can identify them a mile off. Even if you can't see the black and white flashing, that round-winged, floppy-flappy style is unmistakable. Not that they can't move pretty quickly when they want to.

The flock above me was fleeing fast, and it was travelling high. I had a feeling that they had already come some way. Probably they were Continental birds, from 'the Low Countries', where the snow and ice was already biting. They had crossed the eastern Channel, decided not to hang around in southern England, where the snow was soon due to follow them, but instead were resolved to carry on down to the milder regions of the south-west, or possibly over to Ireland. During the following hour and a half, the first flock was followed by several others. Some of them were forced quite low as they got caught up in a brief snow flurry, but the majority was flying so high I could hardly see them. I no doubt missed many others, but I kept staring. I was hoping for 'something else', and I knew exactly what that was. Whenever you come across a big Lapwing flock in the country or at the coast, you scan through it in the hope that there might be Golden Plovers attached. There often are. Sometimes there are hundreds, sometimes just a few. I would have settled for one. It was a species I had never seen over the Heath.

Lapwings.

At 11.25 precisely I broke my duck. Or rather, my Golden Plover. It wasn't a lot, but it was more than one. A squadron of ten, way up in the blue, racing westward in a formation and at a speed that would have done credit to the Red Arrows. Golden Arrows, in fact.

It wasn't the end of the year but, for me, it was one of the highlights.

SUMMARY

So that was a year on Hampstead Heath, my local patch.

As a year, 1995 was pretty good, though probably that is as much thanks to the regular coverage from Mark, Peter and myself as the fact that the birds are getting better. Indeed, sadly, there is plenty of evidence that the breeding birds at least are diminishing, which makes it all the more exciting when we gain a species, like the Common Terns (see page 137). Fortunately, not much can prevent migrants from flying over and occasionally dropping in. This year these have included lots of local rarities, several nationally scarce birds, and one full national rarity, whose name escapes me for the moment, but which I'll probably remember next Father's Day.

Every visit and every bird were recorded by the three of us. We all have our different methods of keeping records. I write up a fairly full diary-like log-book, which may include

Golden Plovers.

the odd sketch or photograph. Peter ticks off species and notes numbers in columns in a checklist. Mark uses a computer. This helps him to edit and organize the masses of information that he eventually publishes in the Hampstead Heath annual bird report.

The total number of species recorded on the Heath in 1995 was 116. This is not a huge number, but for an inland location with no large stretches of water, it is pretty good. There are local patches that will record fewer. There are also lots that will record many more. If you already cover such an area, I'm sure you appreciate it. If you don't, I hope you will feel inspired to start.

Oh... but don't bother with Hampstead Heath. Find your own.

By the way, the reason I have devoted so many pages to this is quite simple. The laws and lessons of local patch-watching apply to *all* bird-watching. Where you live is where you learn. Some people never want to go anywhere else.

SOME KEY POINTS FOR LOCAL PATCH-WATCHING

- Try to find somewhere with a variety of habitats.
- Visit it regularly.
- Get out early, and possibly late as well.
- Go out in bad weather.
- Keep an eye on the weather maps for promising conditions.
- Keep to a fairly consistent circuit.
- Keep looking up.
- Use your ears.
- Keep a record of everything.
- Note the arrival and departure dates of migrants.
- Pass records on to local or county bird clubs.
- Re-read your own notebooks now and again.
- Get involved in local conservation issues.
- Enjoy.

8 Big Days Out

I have titled this section 'big days out'. It strikes me that there are basically two possible approaches here. There is the excursion – a day, or maybe a weekend – that has a goal or target of seeing a particular species, or group of species. It is a sort of quest, that gives a purpose

King Eider – the 'Queen' isn't anything like as lovely.

to your birdwatching. At the extreme end is twitching – going to see one particular rare bird. Usually, though, it is more a search for an experience. It could involve a specialized habitat and the associated species – moorland, sea cliffs or an estuary, perhaps – or it could be a region. One of my most enjoyable expeditions was a few days spent touring eastern Scotland in search of the various Scottish specialities: Capercaillie, Ptarmigan, Crested Tit, Golden Eagle and so on. It was on that trip that I also managed to see the bird I had promised myself since my first visit to Slimbridge: a stunningly handsome male King Eider, bobbing along in the middle of a flotilla of its commoner cousins.

I shall come to the second approach to a 'big day out' later in this chapter. Meanwhile, let's go on a wild goose chase.

WILD GOOSE CHASES

Heaven knows, you'd think geese would be easy enough to see. They are big, extremely noisy, and they tend to go around in enormous flocks. Whoever coined the phrase a 'wild goose chase' must have been a birder. It could have been me.

Just about everyone has heard of the Wildfowl and Wetlands Trust (WWT, see page 214). As a bird organization its fame is probably second only to the RSPB's. The Trust's headquarters are at Slimbridge in Gloucestershire, alongside the River Severn, and they are pretty well known too, being amongst the country's most popular visitor attractions, not just for birdwatchers but for family outings and school trips. You may well have been there, in which case you'll know what a fantastic place it is. It is a huge complex with lots of buildings: staff accommodation, administration offices, research laboratories, teaching facilities, an information centre, gift shop and restaurant. There is also a massive area housing the captive birds: lakes, marshes and pens, all connected by a network of immaculately signposted walkways, plus the secret breeding areas behind the scenes, where birds are reared for reintroduction into the wild. Then there is 'the wild' itself: the vast expanses of mudflats and water meadows alongside the estuary known as the Dumbles, overlooked by a number of impressive hides which allow views of the sometimes thousands of wild geese, ducks and swans that winter there each year. Yes, Slimbridge is an elaborate and impressive place. But it hasn't always been like this.

Back in 1945, when Peter Scott was scanning through the flocks of Whitefronted Geese and spotted a lone Lesser Whitefront (at that time, only the third British record), he was inspired to make a dream come true. A year later he set up the Severn Wildfowl Trust at Slimbridge.

Ten years after that, in 1956, when I was fifteen, I paid my first visit. Not an historic occasion, I admit, but it was for me! I had persuaded my dad to make the then rather slow, long drive down from Birmingham so that I could go on my first wild goose chase. But first, there were the captive birds. We paid our modest entrance fee at the reception kiosk, which in those days was little more than a wooden hut. There were nothing like the numbers of birds that there are today, but nevertheless it still constituted – to quote the leaflet – 'the most comprehensive wild-fowl collection in the world'. I remember that phrase so well because I used it in a 'what I did this weekend' essay at school, and my English teacher underlined 'comprehensive' and put a '?' by it, as if it was the wrong word. It wasn't. 'Comprehensive' means 'all-inclusive'. To be fair, I suppose that was a bit of an exaggeration. There wasn't a specimen of every single duck, goose and swan in the world at the Trust, but there were quite a lot. There were certainly plenty of species that delighted me.

As we wandered round the pens, I enjoyed close-up views of birds that, up till then, I had only seen at a distance. I particularly remember male Smews, looking as if they had been cast in pure white porcelain, and then dropped and been mended, leaving them with delicate black crack-lines on their bodies. The closest I'd got to one previously was a single bird, seen through a snow-storm, half a mile away across my local reservoir. I also relished the opportunity to study 'difficult' species. I compared female Teal with Garganey, and Scaup with Tufted Duck. In both cases, I confirmed

Male Smew.

| Female Tufted Duck. | Female Scaup. | Female Teal. | Female Garganey. |

an almost failsafe birdwatching rule: 'If you are not sure if the bird is the rare one, it probably isn't!' It doesn't matter how much white there is round the base of the bill, a female Tufted just isn't a Scaup. The species have different 'jizzes'. In fact, it is the same with almost all female ducks. Many of them are very similar plumage-wise – basically dull and brown – but they can be identified merely by their shapes. The collection was a great place to learn and practise.

It was also a great place to marvel at species that I promised myself I would someday see in the wild. King Eider really impressed me. I wondered if Dad would fancy a drive up to Scotland some weekend to search for one. Or Hooded Mergansers – they were very pretty – how about a holiday in Canada, Dad?

Meanwhile, there was a more immediate opportunity of putting theory into practice. I turned my attention to the British geese. There was a whole penful of them, all lined up for instant comparisons. They obviously weren't 'easy'. Even only a few yards away, the 'grey geese' in particular all looked remarkably similar. Whitefronts, Grey Lags, Pinkfeet, Bean Geese, all basically greyish, with shades of brown, some bits a little darker, some a little paler perhaps. I took a deep breath and tried to remember what I'd learnt from the books. 'Legs and beak colours are very important.' OK. So I checked those. Pinkfeet have pink feet. Fair enough. On the end of pink legs. But so had the Grey Lags. (So what are 'lags'? Obviously not a misprint for 'legs'!) However, the Grey Lags had largely pink beaks too, whilst the Pinkfeet's were mainly brown. And what about the Whitefronts? They also had pink beaks – unless they were Greenland Whitefronts, in which case they were orange. And where was the 'white front'? Just a little patch on the forehead, that's where. Unless it was a juvenile, in which case, it wasn't white at all. These names really weren't very helpful. How about wing patterns? I seemed to recall that they were important points in identification. I was thinking this when one of the Trust staff came out and scattered grain on the path, and was almost knocked sideways by a squawking stampede of mixed goose species, all flapping their wings wildly to reveal that – in many cases – they hardly had any. The flight feathers had been clipped to make sure that they didn't escape. Fair enough, but it hardly helped my identification studies.

It also reminded me that there were genuine wild geese to be chased and time was getting short. I left Dad having a nap in the car, and headed for the Dumbles, or rather to the hides overlooking them. In those days, as I recall, there were only two or three hides. I followed the path down to one of them, peered through the window and saw nothing at all. So I moved to the next. Again I saw nothing. Not only was I disappointed, I almost felt like complaining. Back at the entrance, there had been an information blackboard: 'Wild geese, from the hides. 3000 Whitefronts. Plus 15 Pinkfeet, 4 Beans, and 1 Lesser Whitefront.' It looked like a menu in a bistro. Surely they were guaranteed? So where were they? Or were wild geese 'off' today?

There was one more hide I could try. I walked back through the pens and climbed the stairs of the Tower Hide. Nowadays, it is very tall and sturdy; back then, it was less tall and distinctly rickety. Nevertheless, it would surely afford a panoramic view, which would include the huge goose flock. It did. But it wasn't quite the unforgettable experience I had anticipated. The vista was indeed vast. On either side, empty green fields stretched away until they were dissolved by the mist. Ahead, across what had to be nearly a mile of more birdless turf, was the River Severn. It was low tide. Where presumably there was sometimes water, there were now acres and acres of mud. The visibility wasn't good and – even through my binoculars – I could barely see the far side of the river. I could, however, just about decipher the paler line of several sand-banks out in the middle. On them were darker lines and blotches that just might have been moving. I pulled out my trusty old brass telescope. There were no new-fangled compact lightweight spotting scopes back in the fifties. We had to make do with the sort of antiquated optics that Nelson clapped his blind eye to. I too saw no ships, but I did see geese. Well, I thought they were geese. To be honest, at this distance, they were little more than fuzzy blobs, but there were lots of them and they were definitely alive. I scanned along the line, eliminating other possibilities. Cormorants? No, too hunched, and they looked as if they were shuffling along and occasionally probing the mud. Waders then? Curlews maybe? No, come on, even at this range I would surely be able to make out a foot-long down-curved beak! They were wildfowl. But could they be ducks? Wigeon perhaps: they snuffle about on mud in large flocks. 'No,' I reasoned, 'They are not Wigeon, because *those* are Wigeon – a small party of them just in front of the blobs – and they are definitely much smaller.' Thus I was convinced – I was indeed looking at my first flock of wild geese. They were presumably Whitefronts but, at this distance and in this light, they were black all over. There were certainly at least 1000 out there, so they *had* to be Whitefronts. Nevertheless, the evidence was purely circumstantial. Could I tick them? Or did I need a better view?

It was then that I was tempted. I had just about convinced myself that it was highly unlikely that there had been a sudden influx of 1000 Pinkfeet, or Grey Lags, or indeed Lesser Whitefronts, or any other grey goose species that would have been equally unidentifiable at such a distance, and therefore I could add Whitefront to my list with certainty, when my identification was confirmed. Even as I gave the blobs a last glance through my scope, a head popped up from under the cover of the river-bank. It was still a very long way away, but it was a lot closer than the birds out on the mud. It was also undeniably a goose. What's more, it had a white forehead, which it flashed for hardly a second, before popping back down out of sight. I waited for it to pop up again. But it didn't. I should have been grateful and content. But no. I had had a little taste and I wanted more. The bird was surely not alone. Indeed, since I could see no other geese except the 1000 blobs, I was now convinced that no fewer than 2000 Whitefronts and probably other species – the balance of the flock on the blackboard menu – were feeding just out of sight under the lip of the river-bank: the bank that was so much closer to me than the mudflats out in the river; the bank that could surely be reached by approaching it under cover of the hedge that seemed to start only about a hundred yards beyond the perimeter fence of the Trust enclosure; the bank that was definitely 'out of bounds'.

I am probably risking being struck off membership of the WWT, but I hereby confess that, on that grey late afternoon in January 1956, I trespassed. I felt guilty then, and I feel guilty now. What makes the guilt even less easy to bear is that my misdemeanour not only went unpunished, it was rewarded. Crime *did* pay. I timed my run exquis-itely. It was getting quite late in the afternoon, at a time when most of the visitors had gone home and the tame geese were expecting their tea. I waited till the bloke feeding them had been obliterated by a deluge of ravenous honkers, and dashed off down the lane that I felt must lead to the Dumbles. In fact, it led to a five-bar gate. It was locked – which made me feel bad – but I noticed that tyre tracks passed through it, which made me feel better. It is sad how reason comes to the aid of felony. 'If the geese can put up with the odd trac-tor without it freaking them, they can put up with the occasional schoolboy,' I told myself. I needed no longer than the time I took to justify the move to vault over the gate and sprint the hundred yards to the beginning of the hedge. I was spattered with mud, out of breath and feeling the sort of fear only a schoolboy knows, but I had made it so far and there was no going back. I did, however, look back every now and then as I scuttled along the hawthorn, and was relieved not to see the glint of binoculars from the Tower Hide. Nevertheless, when I reached the end of the hedge, I threw myself to the ground and crawled the next fifty yards or so along a soaking wet ditch. Finally, I reached the cover of what looked like the ruins of an old gun-site or wartime shelter. It struck me as rather appropriate since I had to accept that I could hardly complain were I to be spotted by a Trust warden and blasted with a twelve-bore.

There was no gunshot, but the scene was by no means silent. I was aware of my own heavy breathing and the thumping of my heart, and the hissing of the wind. But, through all that, I heard sounds that instantly banished any thoughts I had that I was doing the wrong thing. I was now less than twenty yards from the edge of the river. From where I was crouched, I couldn't actually see the water – or rather the mud – and I couldn't see any birds. But I could hear them. The calls of Curlews, the whistles of Wigeon and, most thrilling and unforgettable of all, the sounds of the wild geese.

It is almost impossible to transcribe goose noises. The field guides try, but the phonetics are so inadequate as to be almost comic: 'Kow-yoo', 'Krang ung ung', 'Dyeee-yik'! Even onomatopoeic similes don't help: 'whinnying', 'yelping'. None of them captures the magic. There is music in a single goose call that no words can express. A whole flock is a veritable symphony, except that that word implies too much organization. It is as if the birds are talking to each other, maybe singing, maybe celebrating, maybe affirming that they belong together. It is a primitive sound, tribal, absolutely full of life. In a word: wild!

As I knelt forward to peer over the edge of the river-bank, I was surrounded by that sound. Goose necks popped up in alarm – not one but many, many more. I had been right. Maybe there weren't 2000, but there certainly were an awful lot. Whether they saw me, or merely sensed my presence, I don't know, but they began shuffling out on to the mud. My binoculars trembled with excitement as I began to scan through them, trying to check the identification features. Whitefronts: adults – easy – juveniles, lacking the white foreheads and black belly bars, but the same jizz. And what's that one? Smaller, darker neck. A Pinkfoot? Or could it be a juvenile Lesser? Oh, come on, I couldn't be *that* lucky! I began to panic. I really didn't know my grey geese well enough. I was strangely relieved when the birds began panicking too. Forget identification, just enjoy. First a few, then wave after wave took to the air. The noise was almost deafening, and totally wonderful. Instead of flying directly away from me, many of them wheeled over my head and then swung inland.

As the mudflats became deserted, I noticed that the tide was coming in quite rapidly. Maybe it was the advancing water that had made them take off like that. Maybe I hadn't scared them after all. Maybe I was just trying to kid myself. In any event, the geese were now pitching down in the field, right in front of the Tower Hide. What's more, the blobs from the river were flying in to join them. Maybe that was the place where they always roosted. If I had stayed in the hide, I would have had a fantastic view, and I wouldn't have had to trespass at all. Maybe.

I waited till it was almost dark before scurrying back along the hedge, over the gate and through the Trust exit, which was being closed up for the night. The man who had been feeding the tame geese gave me a funny look, as if wondering why he hadn't noticed me round the pens for the past hour, but before he had time to translate his thoughts into any kind of cross-questioning, I was in Dad's car and heading back to Birmingham. It was the end of my first wild goose chase and it had been successful. It would not be the last, and not all of them would prove such a success.

Well, not immediately.

My first trip to the Solway Firth reinforced a fact: wild geese may be faithful to traditional wintering grounds but that doesn't mean they stick to the same few fields. Birds that have flown thousands of miles from Russia or Greenland think little of wandering round a bit when they get to Britain. I discovered that the Solway region had about half-a-dozen favoured locations. They were all within a few miles of each other, but it was perfectly possible for an anxious motorized bird-watcher – driving my own car by now – to 'lose' huge flocks of geese for days on end. Sometimes you are in the wrong place at the wrong time; or sometimes the birds are simply 'hiding', down in a dip or behind a hill. On that trip, it took me three days to find 6000 Barnacle Geese, and nearly a week to catch up with my ultimate quarry: a party of fifteen Bean Geese.

In fact, the Solway experience typified the attraction of goose chasing. It is partly the thrill of the big flocks of birds, and partly the challenge of finding the occasional 'odd ones'. This can be a real 'needle in a haystack' job, even when the rarity you are looking for is supposedly conspicuous as, for example, a Snow Goose. There are, alas, quite a number of Snow Geese that have managed to regrow previously clipped flight feathers and escape from less carefully kept collections than the Wildfowl Trust. However, if you have set your heart on seeing a genuine wild Canadian-grown Snow Goose this side of the Atlantic, your best bet is probably to go to southern Ireland. Thus I made several trips to County Wexford to visit the Slobs. No, not the family from the *Harry Enfield's Television Programme*, the goose grounds. The North and South Slobs are where I have had the best views of wild geese anywhere in the world. I'm not sure if the arrangement is still the same now but when I went there, you were allowed – or rather instructed – to use your car as a mobile hide. Thus, on a crisp February day, I found myself driving along past fields full of Greenland Whitefronts searching for the three 'real' Canada Geese and the Snow Goose that had been reported that winter.

I soon found the Canadas. One of them looked pretty similar to the ones that swim around just about any park lake in England, but the other two looked distinctly authentic. One was very big and the other was very small. In fact there are several 'races' of Canada Goose. It is a complicated business, and certainly not worth delving into here. Suffice it to say that these birds, in the company of several thousand Greenland Whitefronts, were almost certainly carrying Canadian passports. It didn't make them separate tickable species, but it did make them rather exciting.

But what about that Snow Goose? That was proving rather harder to find. There were plenty of large white birds dotted around the Slobs that day but they all turned out to be swans, albeit satisfyingly wild ones: both Whoopers and Bewicks, for instant comparison. However, it wasn't actually a pure white bird I was looking for. The bird that had been reported was a 'blue phase' Snow Goose and, if that sounds confusing, to make matters worse it certainly isn't blue. The body of the bird is sort of greyish-brown, and the head is the only bit that is white. Since wild geese spend much of their time with their heads down, nibbling grass, hidden by the birds around them, it wasn't going to be easy to find. Nevertheless, eventually, I did pick it out. Or so I thought. I certainly saw a goose with a white head. In fact I saw two. And I made careful sketches of them. However, when I showed them to the Warden he confirmed what I had suspected at the back of my mind, but was trying to suppress. Both the white-headed geese were hybrids: living proof of the fact that it isn't only wildfowl in collections that have a habit of interbreeding and producing youngsters that display a bit of this and a bit of that, as a consequence of parents who couldn't resist a bit of the other! If you see a duck or a goose that you can't find in the book, it is not a bad rule to conclude that it may well be a hybrid. Some birdwatchers hate these but it is actually quite fun sorting them out. In the case of my two white-headed geese, one was considered to be the offspring of a Canada and a Whitefront, whilst the other was probably a Whitefront with a bit of

Nasty hybrids.

A real Blue Goose.

Snow Goose in it. But not enough. I couldn't count it. Fortunately, on a later visit, I did catch up with a pure Snow Goose, albeit a blue phase.

And so the wild goose chases have continued. The thrill of the numbers and the noise has never diminished, whether it be Pinkfeet in Scotland, Brents in Norfolk, or indeed Magpie Geese in Australia. I have also been lucky enough to tick off the few 'odd ones' that we get in Britain, such as the exquisite little Red-breasted Goose that looks as if it has been painted by an art nouveau designer. However, one rare goose eluded me for years: the Lesser Whitefront. It was the species that had inspired Peter Scott to found the Wildfowl Trust and, appropriately, it lured me back there winter after winter, year after year.

Even more appropriately, it was in Sir Peter's company that I finally saw the bird. Again, I was on 'private ground', but this time I didn't have to trespass. Late in 1982, I received a letter from Sir Peter inviting me to visit Slimbridge, with a view to my enjoying the geese and becoming a council member of the Trust. I was immensely honoured and delighted to accept both invitations. The long-term satisfaction has been a closer association with a wonderful organization (an association which I hope will continue despite my confession!). The short-term reward was scanning the Dumbles with my telescope, alongside the great man, trying to pick out a Lesser Whitefront which we both knew was out there somewhere. Sir Peter offered to find it for me. I hope he wasn't offended when I said I'd prefer to find it for myself. Actually, I'm sure he understood perfectly. When I eventually did spot the bird, his smile was almost as broad as mine.

Most birdwatchers will agree that there is something special about finding your own birds, but you don't have to! In fact, wild goose chasing is generally a much less risky business these days. Happily there are very few goose grounds that aren't safe sanctuaries, administered by the WWT, or the RSPB, or the Irish Wildbird Conservancy. The viewing facilities are often superb, with skyscraper-height hides, picture windows, and permanent giant telescopes or binoculars. In a sense, you are shown the birds. Of course, wildfowl can still be uncooperative,

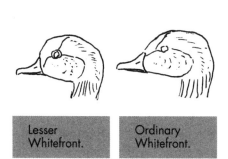

Lesser
Whitefront.

Ordinary
Whitefront.

but even then you can probably enjoy them on video at the information centre. These reserves are terrific value, for birds and birdwatchers. A perfect way of enjoying a 'big day out' experience.

There is, however, another approach to the big day out: you simply try to see as many species as possible. What you are after is not a particular

species or spectacle, but maximum variety. You could call it 'making the most of your birding'.

Ptarmigan – one of the Scottish quest species.

If you want a really big day out, you could try... a bird race.

BIRD RACING

So what is a bird race? Well, it is nothing to do with Daffy Duck in a sports car, or even homing pigeons. It is a race between birdwatchers. The idea is simple. Most races take place over a period of a single day, usually from midnight to midnight. During the twenty-four hours, you and your team have to record as many species as possible (identification can be based on hearing as well as seeing the birds). Normally, there are four birders in each team: three out of four have to confirm the identification of the bird for it to count. In fact, the fourth member is often the recorder, whose main job is to keep the list up to date. The primary reason for the recent popularity of bird racing in Britain has been to raise money for wildlife charities. The simplest and perhaps the most challenging way is for each team to be sponsored so much per species. So the more you see the more you make.

There is, however – perhaps surprisingly – a long and elaborate history to bird racing. It probably began in the United States, sometime fairly early in the century, when several American birders got into the habit of keeping 'big day' lists. By the late 1920s, they had begun forming teams and competing against each other. For many years, the events continued merely as exercises in competitiveness and kudos, and it wasn't until the late 1970s that some imaginative entrepreneur hit upon the idea of sponsorship. Meanwhile, on this side of the Atlantic, the same sort of process occurred. 'Big days' for fun evolved into effective fund-raising by the early 1980s, and they have now grown into the annual massive, nationwide County Bird Race, in which literally hundreds of teams take part. They compete for a splendidly diverse range of awards that encourage everyone to have a go – from absolute beginners to seasoned 'professionals' – and allow for all kind of transport, from fast cars to bikes and horses.

Bird racing goes on all across the world. Sometimes the distances travelled during the twenty-four hours are immense, sometimes very restricted: from crossing Kenya via a network of carefully timed cars, boats and small planes to sticking within the confines of the M25 in London. What's more, the media have often followed the racers, recording the fun and frustrations for radio, television and newspapers. If you would like to read a full-blown account of bird racing and what it involves, I can only immodestly recommend a book I helped to write: *The Big Bird Race* by Bill Oddie and David Tomlinson (Collins). It is out of print now, but you may well be able to pick up a copy from a specialist natural history book service or even from a library. Heaven knows, I would enjoy rewriting and expanding on it for this book, but it would take another couple of hundred pages!

Meanwhile, why have I brought up the subject? Well, as you will have gathered, I am a great fan of bird races: they raise a lot of money and they are great fun, and if you ever get a chance to take part in one I really do suggest you should have a go. Even if you feel you are not quite ready for that sort of hectic activity yet, the principles involved in bird racing can teach you a lot of very valuable lessons about the techniques of birdwatching, which will help you enjoy your own 'big days out'.

On a race, you are trying to record as many species as possible within a very short time. It therefore follows that your birdwatching has to be ultra-efficient. The principles that apply to a race can also be applied to any birding day out, or to a weekend, or a fortnight, or indeed a lifetime – but at a rather more leisurely pace!

THE PRINCIPLES OF BIRD RACING

First principle: get up early. The dawn chorus is a wonderful aural treat and, as it happens, it gives you a great start to the day's list, as species after species bursts into song.

Second principle: learn to use your ears to recognize songs and calls.

Third principle: during the day, cover as many habitats as possible to see different species.

Fourth principle: make sure you see everything there is to be seen in each particular place. This means constantly asking yourself: 'What do I expect to see here?' and making sure you do. Also, if you are aware of the common birds, you will more easily spot the odd one out... the one that 'shouldn't' be there.

Fifth principle: plan your day so you are at the right place at the right time – in the woods for the dawn chorus, at the estuary for the oncoming tide, on the heath at dusk, and so on.

THE ITINERARY

The secret of so much birding is the timing. Perhaps I can best illustrate this by giving an example of what a theoretical 'big day' itinerary might look like.

Time of the year: May. This is the most favoured month for bird races, since spring migrants have arrived and are singing to establish territories, whilst there may still be a few lingering winter visitors, plus – if an east wind blows – it might bring in some rarities. (Having said that, you can do a bird race at any time of the year and the same kind of route would be largely appropriate.)

We will assume we are birding in a county near the coast. So the plan would be...

Pre-dawn: In the woods, listening for owls (see page 54).

Dawn: The dawn chorus. Not only are the first bursts of song easiest to identify, the birds are often most active early in the morning and easier to see as well.

Early morning: At the coast, seawatching (see page 58). For 'fly by' auks, sea ducks, terns, skuas or even shearwaters. Movement at sea is almost invariably better early in the day and can wane completely by mid-morning.

172 BIG DAYS OUT

The middle of the day: Lakes, reservoirs, gravel-pits (see page 55), for wildfowl, grebes, Reed and Sedge Warblers. Activity tends to be fairly constant throughout the day at these habitats.

Also visit specific sites for particular birds: for example, a stream known to hold Grey Wagtail or Kingfisher.

Late afternoon: The estuary (see page 58). The tide is rising, covering the mudflats and thus concentrating the waders and making them easier to sort through.

Dusk: In heathland and nearby woods (see page 55). For Woodcock, Nightingale, Nightjar, and often a late burst of song, or birds calling as they fly off to roost.

OK. So that's how it *could* be if it all went well!

Of course, the truth is that various uncontrollable factors may affect the 'ideal' day. For example, high tide might be early in the morning, which could disrupt your dawn schedule. This tends to be one of the most frustrating facts about birding: *most* places are best early in the morning, and you can't be everywhere at the same time!

Also, there is the weather. If it is a dull wet dawn, the birds won't sing so heartily – if at all! Or the fog could roll in and obliterate the estuary entirely. Or your car could break down or get involved in road-works. I suppose I should add one final principle to the others I listed above; be flexible! Be prepared to change your plans depending on the weather, or the traffic, or indeed on which birds you most want to see when time is running out!

Anyway, I really mustn't go on too much about this bird race obsession of mine. I hope, though, I have got over the message I am trying to convey. You don't have to be actually taking part in a race against the clock or other birders, but... when you go out for a day's birding and you want to see as many species as possible, how about at least pretending you are taking part in a race? Plan and follow the optimum route and schedule, and keep a list of what you record. It doesn't have to be for the full twenty-four hours of course. You could try it for just a morning or afternoon.

In fact, for several years, I and three birding friends used to make a habit of meeting up for Sunday lunch in mid-May in the middle of Kent, and then walking off our heavy meal with a two-hour mini-bird race round the local countryside. On foot, and stuffed with Yorkshire

pudding, we rarely covered a vast area of ground but, by thoroughly checking the available habitats – woods, farmyard, duck pond, fields

One Dotterel is pretty enough – so now imagine another eleven.

– we usually racked up around fifty species, an incredible number given the area covered. On one occasion this included a delightful 'trip' of a dozen Dotterel, a new species for the bloke whose house we were visiting. The birds were in a field of spring wheat, directly opposite his kitchen window, but I am absolutely certain that had we not been scanning so meticulously for Lapwing or Partridges, we would never have noticed the Dotterels crouching, barely visible and almost silent, down in the furrows.

BRANCHING FURTHER OUT

FAIR ISLE

Sadly, nowadays, it seems that fewer and fewer birders are prepared to 'risk' staying in one place for a week or more, preferring to follow the calls of their pagers or Birdline in pursuit of rarities. It is a pity because, undoubtedly, many of my happiest memories are of 'birding holidays' to various places in Britain, some of them, like Fair Isle, pretty remote. When I was a schoolboy, I lived in Birmingham. No dis-respect to the Second City, but it is an awful long way from the sea. The vast majority of my local birdwatching was done at various Midland reservoirs. Over the years, I did see several 'seabirds' at some of them. Gulls, of course – plenty of those – terns occasionally, a few divers, even a single Eider Duck, but I longed for the 'real thing'. What's more, other young (but older than me) birdwatchers in our school Natural History Society taunted me with tales of faraway places where they'd seen not only lots of seabirds, but also various rare migrants that I hadn't even heard of. They told me that these places were official Bird Observatories and that if I wanted to qualify as a proper birdwatcher, I really ought to go and stay at some of them. So I did. Along with a couple of friends, I visited Dungeness in Kent and Monk's House up in Northumberland, opposite the Farne Islands. It was the latter that really captured my imagination and enthusiasm, and introduced me to three elements of birding that became immediate obsessions: seabirds, trapping and ringing, and small islands. My idea of heaven would be a place that combined all three. In 1959 I found that place.

Most people have heard of Fair Isle, even if only on the shipping forecast – 'Dogger and Fair Isle, wind south-west gale force 9. Good sailing gentlemen' – or as a knitting pattern, featuring especially on cardigans worn by small boys in black and white photography. In fact, I've got a snap of me wearing one. (Oops, giving my age away again.) But did you know that Fair Isle is also the site of Britain's first and still most famous Bird Observatory? Well, that's what I was told sometime back in the late fifties, and I immediately resolved to go there. I had just ended the final term of my last full year at school. I'd managed to wangle myself a place at university and, as a reward, my dad said that he would pay for my dream trip. Of course, he thereby also got rid of me for a fortnight during the long summer holidays, so no doubt he considered it money well spent. Indeed it was.

In fact, the travel must have cost quite a bit. It was a long journey. On August 17th, I and a couple of birding chums caught an early morning train from Birmingham to Aberdeen. We were on it for most of the day. Then, at half past four in the afternoon, we boarded a steamship and began sailing up the east coast of Scotland. We spent the last few hours of daylight gazing across the waves, watching Guillemots and Razorbills tazzing by like little pied torpedoes, and hoping to spot a shearwater or two. In fact we spotted two different species: first, a small group of Manx, and then a single Sooty Shearwater. The latter lived up to its name rather well. It definitely sheered over the water, and its plumage was indeed sooty, which made it easy to pick out amongst the black and white Manxies. My first new bird of the trip. I was so excited I was definitely going to have trouble getting to sleep that night. I made myself a pillow from my rucksack, stretched out on deck and stared at the stars until the gentle roll of the boat eventually made me doze off. I awoke shivering, aware that the temperature had dropped a few degrees. This was to be expected. After all, we had travelled northwards all night, past the tip of Scotland and past the Orkney Islands, and we were now halfway up the Mainland of Shetland. As I lay there, I could just make out the coastline on my right, to the west. On my left, there was open sea. Above me, there were birds. Gulls, yes, I'd expect those, but also something much darker: chocolate-brown, except for dazzling white flashes on its wings that seemed to glow in the early morning light. A Great Skua. I'd seen a couple flying by off Monk's House one autumn, half a mile out to sea, but here was one circling

Next page Majestic cliffs and cosy crofts.

just above my head as if it were considering me for breakfast. I stood up, and it veered away over the waves. As my eyes followed it, I picked out a couple of birds on the water only a few yards from the ship. Auks, yes; Guillemots, yes again. But not the common ones. These were all black, with white wing patches. Put into words, it amounted to much the same description as the Skua! But this was a completely different bird. Neat, petite, with scarlet feet. A little poem, no less, all adding up to my first close-up views of Black Guillemots. Within minutes of opening my eyes, I had enjoyed stunning views of two Shetland specialities. 'Black Guillemot and Great Skua,' I repeated to a curious fellow traveller who had asked me what I was looking at. 'Ah, Tystie and Bonxie,' he corrected me, in a strong Shetland accent that sounded more like Scandinavian than Scots. It was my first lesson in local names. I've never used anything else since.

We docked in Lerwick – the capital of Shetland, and its only really sizeable town – in time for a late breakfast. Shortly after midday, we were on a bus heading back down Mainland towards Sumburgh at the southernmost tip. Most of the terrain was bleak, treeless and apparently fairly birdless too, except for the occasional Wheatear by the roadside and more Skuas in the sky. As we travelled down the eastern coast, we were never out of sight of the sea. After about an hour's journey we passed

Tystie looking justifiably worried by the attentions of a Bonxie.

the 'Sumburgh' sign and saw the ocean stretching further southwards. Somewhere out there, over twenty-odd miles of ominously grey and choppy water, was Fair Isle.

We were dropped off at Grutness Pier and told to wait for the *Good Shepherd*. The *Good Shepherd* was not a person but a small boat, its name not inappropriate as we found ourselves sharing it with a flock of sheep. In fact, we wouldn't have minded cuddling up to them as, by this time, the wind was freshening and it was pretty chilly once we'd chugged out of the lee of the headland. It also began spitting with rain, and consequently we spent most of the journey sheltering under a tarpaulin, which was the only cover available. It was about an hour and a half later that a ray of sunlight broke through the clouds, lured us out and illuminated our first view of our final destination.

The north end of the island loomed above us. It looked pretty forbidding. A sheer cliff rose literally hundreds of feet and, around its base, the sea churned and half-submerged rocks appeared and disappeared as the swell rose and fell. On top of the cliff was a lighthouse, a testimony to the obvious fact that these were very dangerous waters. Indeed, we wondered if the island had been christened in a spirit of sarcasm by mariners who had perhaps survived one of the many shipwrecks. Fair Isle indeed!

However, as we carried on past the north end, the waters began to calm down until finally the boat swung to the right – sorry, starboard – and glided serenely into a small sheltered harbour that was almost dead calm. There was a tiny jetty and even a golden crescent of sand. The skipper told us it was called North Haven. Good name. As we tottered ashore, it wasn't hard to imagine the relief and safety this place must have provided for anyone who had been tossed on the tempestuous seas round Shetland. The difference between death and survival, hell and heaven. Fair Isle indeed.

We were there at last. The journey had taken us the best part of two days. Nowadays, you can fly the whole way and, if you get the connections right, you can eat breakfast in London and lunch on the island. What's more, that midday meal will be served to you in the spacious and airy dining-room of the splendid Observatory building often – justifiably – referred to by visitors as the birdwatcher's Hilton.

Back in 1959, however, things weren't quite so luxurious. The Observatory was housed in a small huddle of ex-naval huts that definitely did not have all mod cons. Not that we bothered to find out immediately. We just dumped our bags and, despite rather wobbly sea legs, set out to explore. We didn't get far and we didn't see that many birds – a small selection of waders on the beaches, plenty of Wheatears and a couple of Whinchats – but it did qualify us to join in the ritual of the evening log. It really did feel like a ritual, and a slightly satanic one at that, as we gathered round a huge cauldron of steaming cocoa, in a room full of shadows lit only by the dim and slightly spooky glow of an oil lamp. In these snug but murky circumstances, the Warden of the Observatory called out the names of the various species that had been recorded on the island that day, and those present – no more than a dozen of us – responded with the numbers and where they had been seen. The Warden then worked out a day total for each species and duly wrote the number into the appropriate column in the log-book. I have a sneaking feeling that he may well have had to write out some of them again the next morning since it was so dark in there that he must surely have made a few mistakes. Nevertheless, what immediately impressed us was that although we were paying visitors – though not paying very much, mind you – we were not merely there on holiday. In a way, we were also there to work. We had immediately been transcripted on to the Observatory team, as it were, and we would be expected to play our part in making sure that the island and its birds were covered efficiently. Far from resenting this in any way, we were flattered. To quote Duke Ellington: it was 'nice work if you can get it'.

Our bedrooms were tiny but cosy, and we took to our sleeping-bags, serenaded by the distant bleating of sheep and the piping of Oystercatchers. The only slightly odd sensation was the feeling that the room was swaying gently, as if we were still at sea, an illusion heightened by the fact that we could hear waves breaking not many yards away. The wind rattling the guy-ropes that steadied the wooden buildings reminded us that we were safely anchored. It was the first time I had spent a night on a small island, surrounded only by sea and natural sounds. I slept wonderfully well.

The next morning, after breakfast and washing up, we set out with an assistant warden to be given a sort of guided tour. It took almost the whole of the day, and made us realize that Fair Isle isn't actually *that* small. Though it may be only about three miles long and a mile across at the widest, by the time you have wandered the length and breadth and criss-crossed several times, checking all the different habitats, and the possible places the birds might get to – which is almost anywhere – you have covered an awful lot of ground. Not that birds were the only fascination on that first day. I was absolutely captivated by the atmosphere of a traditional Shetland community. There were probably no more than about sixty people living on the island. Most of the families were crofters. The word 'croft' seemed to cover both their dwellings and their land. The houses were mostly single storey, with thick stone or concrete walls to keep out the elements. They also had tiny windows, probably for the same reason, but I couldn't help thinking that was a bit of a shame, but then I reflected that since the people spent so much time out of doors anyway, they probably weren't too bothered

Fieldy – excuse the photo but it was taken with a Box Brownie...

about having a lovely view. What's more, it hardly gets light through-out the long northern winter, and, conversely, it barely gets dark during the summer months, so big windows would be inappropriate at either time.

The rest of the croft was the surrounding farmland. Some of it just looked like grassy fields with sheep in them. One had a small herd of cows. Others were planted with vegetables – neeps and tatties (turnips and potatoes) – whilst the largest areas contained crops, such as wheat and barley. As we wandered south, our guide taught us the names of the various crofts and of their respective owners. These invariably consisted of the Christian name only, with the name of the croft replacing the sur-name and coming first. Thus Jerry, whose croft was called Leogh, was referred to as 'Leogh Jerry'. This distinguished him from the Jerry who lived at the Haa and was therefore 'Haa Jerry'. To be honest, I'm not sure I accurately recall all the names now but, at the time, we needed to be told which crofters were 'birdwatcher-friendly'. Just a few resented the intrusion of the Observatory and its visitors, and their land was therefore out of bounds. Most of the islanders, however, were perfectly happy – or indeed rather proud – if a rare bird was discovered in *their* crops. One or two, in fact, were expert birders in their own right. I seem to recall Midway Jimmy as being an excellent observer and recorder. Certainly I'll never forget Fieldy.

Technically, I suppose George Stout of Field should have been called Field George, but maybe he vetoed it himself. It doesn't really work, does it? In any event, everyone knew him as Fieldy. This was the way I was introduced to him back in '59. He was pretty old, well over eighty I'd guess, and it was like meeting a legend. He wore a tight-fitting grey suit and a flat cap, and his face was wrinkled, stubbled and almost toothless. I suspect his hearing wasn't too good, and I could hardly understand a word he said in his broad Shetland dialect. But his eyes still twinkled. And what eyes they were, and indeed had been for many many years. The fact was that Fieldy was one of the world's great bird-watchers. He had always lived on Fair Isle, and indeed it was his obser-vations that had helped to put it on the birdwatching map. Over the years, he had found and identified many a great rarity, including proba-bly several species that were new to Britain. Moreover, many of his records dated back to a time when binoculars and telescopes were almost unheard of and certainly of very poor quality. So how had he proved his rarities? Simple: he shot 'em! It was the only way. That generation of collector naturalists had a saying: 'What's hit is history, what's missed is mystery.' And Fieldy certainly contributed to history, not least because he found it hard to give up his old ways. Mind you, perhaps one couldn't entirely blame him.

The story goes that quite late on in his life, as his hearing and eyesight deteriorated and his imagination possibly increased, the people at the Bird Observatory came to regard many of his rarity claims with growing scepticism. Too often he reported yet another rarity which nobody else could find. Things got to the point where most of his reports were greeted with a polite smile and a nod, but people simply didn't believe them any more. Until, that is, one autumn when Fieldy reported that he had seen a particularly rare pipit near his croft. He told the Observatory Warden, but no one came to see his bird. The next day, he mentioned it again, but again no one came. This went on for a week. Eventually, Fieldy broke his habit of a lifetime and actually walked up the island to the North Haven and marched into the Observatory sitting-room.

Anticipating the reason for the visit, the Warden spoke first:

'Look, Fieldy, no one else has seen the pipit. If you can't prove it, we can't accept it.' Whereupon Fieldy slapped a closed fist on the table, opened his hand out and revealed... the pipit: stone-dead but correctly identified.

The Assistant Warden told us this story as we continued on our round. He also pointed out the wreckage of a Second World War fighter plane. This led to another story. Apparently, the plane was being flown by a member of the German Luftwaffe who had got into trouble somewhere over the North Sea. As it happened, he was a birdwatcher and therefore naturally decided to try and crash-land on Fair Isle. This he managed to do. He was doubly delighted when on getting out of the cockpit he was approached by a man with a pair of binoculars. He was even more thrilled when he realized who it was. You guessed it. Fieldy. It seems that the German had heard of his fame and spoke enough English to greet him – 'Ah, you must be George Stout of Field. I am honoured to meet you' – and he spent the last years of the war birding peacefully on the island. It was hard to believe that the story was true, but I was certainly beginning to see the attraction of the place.

On we walked, past the Post Office at Shirva, the shop at Stackhoul, the Kirk, and so on, learning a little Old Norse as we went. All the natural features on Fair Isle, and indeed throughout the Northern Isles, are referred to by local words, and it is essential to get to know them. Streams are 'burns', sheltered clefts in the cliffs are 'geos', areas of moorland are 'brecks'. In order to keep a proper record of the birds, it is vital to get to know the name of all the locations. This way it is possible to record accurately where the birds are, and make sure that there are no overlaps between different observers. It also makes it easier to direct people when a rarity is found. Nowadays, the Observatory issues visitors with a little postcard-sized map, but back then we just had to rely on our memories.

TRAPPING AND RINGING

Thus the day went by. Birding the island was not a frantic affair. We took our time to greet local people and to enjoy the atmosphere, the views and the company. It was relaxing, yet it was also methodical. Every area was visited and every bird was noted and numbers recorded, paying particular attention to the migrants. This is the principal work of a Bird Observatory: studying migration. A large part of the activity, therefore, involves trapping and ringing. The theory is straightforward enough. A small, lightweight metal ring is fitted round the leg of the bird. On the ring is written a reference number – which has been noted in the ringing log – and an address. In the case of British rings it says: 'Inform British Museum.' The theory is that if the bird is recovered – perhaps retrapped by other ringers or more likely found dead – the finder will return the ring. Eventually, a pattern of various species' movements and migrations emerges. As I write, in the mid-1990s, ornithologists have indeed accumulated a great deal of data and plotted many routes and amazing journeys. It is even argued by some that ringing may be on the point of outliving its usefulness, though I can't actually agree with that myself, as there is undoubtedly still a lot to learn. Certainly, however, back in the late fifties being involved in ringing felt positively pioneering, and it was probably partly this that had inspired me to gain enough experience to qualify as a licensed ringer myself. (It did then – and still does – require a

great deal of supervised training before a licence is issued.)

The Double Dyke Heligoland Trap.

Mind you, I don't think it was just the satisfaction of contributing to science that appealed to me. There was also the thrill of holding birds in your hands, and marvelling at them at close quarters. And there was the challenge of catching them in the first place! I discovered just how well equipped Fair Isle was to do the job, when I was taken on my first trap round. The traps in question were Heligoland traps, so called because they were developed on the German island of Heligoland, where the world's first Bird Observatory was established. (I wonder if that fighter pilot ever landed there?) Basically, the trap is like a huge funnel – maybe as big as seven feet high and fifteen or twenty feet wide at the mouth. It is made from chicken wire. The funnel narrows into a smaller compartment, which can be shut off by closing a wire door, operated by pulling a string. Then, at the very end, comes the trapping-box. This is made of wood, and has a glass window, which appears to the bird as a means of escape. There is also a sleeve to allow the ringer to reach inside the box and take the bird out.

But why should the bird go in in the first place? Well, normally the trap – the giant funnel – is built over a clump of bushes or small trees. The birds naturally shelter in this cover. Then the ringer and his helpers gently drive them further into the trap. When the bird reaches the second compartment, the door is closed so it can't double back and escape. Finally, it is chivvied towards the trapping-box. It usually sees the window and flies into the box, thinking it is the way out. Another string releases a hinged flap, enclosing the bird in the trapping-box. The ringer quickly puts his hand in through the sleeve, removes the bird, pops it into a small draw-stringed bag, and takes it back to the Observatory where it is weighed, measured, ringed and released. The process is quick, careful and meticulously documented. It can also be great fun!

The trap round on Fair Isle also demanded a degree of physical fitness. Since there are no natural trees, bushes or brambles on the island, the Heligolands were built over dry stone walls or across rocky gullies (geos). In the absence of foliage, these are the places where small migrants seek shelter. The round began fairly sedately in the Observatory garden, which at least had a few straggly raspberry canes and a patch of rhubarb for the birds to skulk in. Then, walking south along the only island road, we climbed a stile to arrive at the Double Dyke Trap. This one might have been erected as an easy-to-understand demonstration of the Heligoland trapping principle (see picture on page 185). The Double Dyke was likely to provide us with our first exercise of the day. Small birds flitted ahead of us along the dry stone wall. It was amazing how they could hide inside it. But we couldn't. Therefore, it was more than likely that they would soon become aware that they were being pursued by the ringers. We started off gently enough, but at the moment that a warbler or wheatear landed anywhere near the mouth of the trap, the only way to persuade it to go into it was to race towards it as fast as possible, even if this meant a fifty-yard dash, usually with binoculars and telescopes slapping into sensitive regions.

If driving the Double Dyke got us out of puff, negotiating the Gully could have been incorporated into an Outward Bound course. This involved descending an almost vertical slope into a narrow valley with a small burn running along the bottom. The Observatory staff had planted – or at least constructed – a tiny patch of cover down there. In fact, it consisted of little more than a tangled wire enclosure with a few stunted flowers and defunct Christmas trees in it, but it did attract the occasional bird, which would flutter out as we approached. Sometimes, the bird would fly almost vertically upwards and out of the valley, thus leaving us to give up and climb all the way up again. What was meant to happen was that the bird would fly further up the geo, where it would seek shelter in what became a sort of narrow gorge.

It was quite pretty up there, with a miniature waterfall, a couple of small, marshy, moss-edged pools, and a little fern-like vegetation. It was also quite a long way up. The bird could fly, but we had to scramble up a precarious ladder or get a foothold on the slippery rocks, and – if we had spotted a bird ahead of us – this all had to be done at great speed. It was perfectly possible to slide all the way back down again, and I soon had bruises to prove it. If, however, you made it to the top of the gully, you – and the bird – would discover that it now had a roof on it! This was made of wire stretched between metal girders, and signified that we had arrived inside the gully trap.

With any luck the bird was now caught, once the door to the last compartment had been closed and it had been persuaded to enter the catching-box. Nevertheless, there was still a rather challenging final leap to make across the top of the ravine, which, if you lost your footing, would land you in four feet of ice-cold water. If indeed you did pull a rarity out of the box at the end of that rigmarole, you certainly felt you'd earned it!

The rest of the circuit took us round another half-dozen wall-sited Heligolands, some of them by the road and others entailing a trek across ankle-twisting bog, till finally we ended up at the Plantation. This was – and still is – the only 'woodland' on Fair Isle. It is completely unnatural, and looks it, since it consists of an oddly incongruous small patch of closely planted conifers, almost entirely enclosed by a Heligoland trap. It looked as if it ought to be extremely efficient. The only problem was that the dense cover not only attracted the birds in the first place, it also provided them with the ideal means of escape. I soon got used to the frustration of thinking I'd caught something, only to find an empty box, and a warbler taunting me from back in the trees which I'd just walked through. Sometimes, though, it worked like a charm and, at half past six on that first evening, the Warden invited me to put my hand into the Plantation trapping-box, knowing, I suspect, that what I would pull out would be a new bird for me. It was a Barred Warbler, my first Fair Isle rarity.

The Barred Warbler wasn't the rarest bird we saw or caught on that visit. There was the Booted

Barred Warbler.

Warbler and the Scarlet Rosefinch, both species that flaunt the Trades Descriptions Act, since the one certainly doesn't wear boots and the other is far from scarlet. The warbler gets its name from its slightly paler feet – slippers at best! – and adult male Rosefinches do indeed blush deep red, but not the fawn-coloured juveniles you see in autumn. The other really rare bird was an Arctic Warbler, reminding us of just how far north we were. There were also plenty of commoner migrants, including close-up views of the kind of species you so often only see flying away or skulking: Lapland Bunting, Short-eared Owl, Merlin and Jack Snipe.

The birds were great, but there was so much more to the Fair Isle experience. Throughout the week we got to know the people and the places. We bought sweaters at the knitwear sale in the Hall, we danced at the Ceilidh and we got invited in for tea and shortbread. And, in the evenings, we sipped our cocoa, talked birds and read about past glories in the pages of the Observatory 'chatti logs': a sort of bird diary written up by various visitors over the years, including some of the true pioneers of British ornithology. I considered it a particular honour when, for the last few days, I was allowed to write the entries. It really made me feel as if I belonged. The truth was that by the end of the fortnight I had fallen in love with the Magic Isle.

Since then I have returned several times, not only to Fair Isle, but to other parts of Shetland. Naturally, over the years, some things have changed. As I've already said, the journey has got a lot easier and quicker, though it can still be disrupted by wayward weather. The Observatory accommodation and facilities are much improved, including of course permanent electricity and the attendant luxuries of TV and video. These are undeniably all gains. The losses include the old characters like Fieldy, and perhaps some of the charm of the old traditions. Mind you, I don't suppose the island women would consider it too much of a pity that their hand-knitting industry has now become fully mechanized, with orders coming in from all over the world.

Happily, though, most things do not change. The scenery is still majestic, and the air is still as bracing as ever. And, of course, there are still the birds. In fact, I really don't feel I've done them justice. So allow me to recall just a few of my most indelible memories. They do truly capture for me some of the most magical aspects of birds and bird-watching. Please remember, as you read them, that you too could enjoy such excitement! Mind you, I'm not promising. Very little in birding is absolutely guaranteed...

SEABIRD CITY

That first August trip had certainly satisfied two of my cherished criteria for the ideal bird location: the island had been terrific, and the trapping and ringing fascinating... but what about the seabirds? Autumn is not really the time to appreciate them at their best. Probably the ideal months are June or July.

Seabird colonies are amongst the most impressive and thrilling wildlife spectacles in nature. You may have seen photos in books or films on the telly but, until you visit one, it is impossible truly to appreciate the teeming numbers, the constant activity, the wonderful sounds and the sheer beauty of the birds. It is as if the colony represents the very force of life itself. There are few things more exhilarating than being on top of the cliffs on a clear, crisp spring day, gazing down at a 'seabird city'. It can also be quite dangerous – don't get too close to the edge – and it can also be a bit intimidating. There is so much going on, it is sometimes hard to know where to look. In fact, the feeling of being overwhelmed by the sheer numbers of birds is part of the thrill, but I do sometimes think people miss out on the details and subtleties. To appreciate them takes time. I had been taught this lesson on the Farne Islands when I stayed at Monk's House as a schoolboy. On my first June visit to Fair Isle, it stood me in good stead.

For literally hours on end I would lie on the clifftop – it's far safer and less conspicuous in that position – taking in every aspect of the scene below. I allowed my eyes to start at the bottom and work their way up. At the foot of the cliff, the seas swirl and eddy, an almost hypnotic effect in itself. On the spray-spattered rocks there would be Eider Ducks. Even above the sound of the surf I could hear the males calling. The sound they make is utterly unduck-like. Not a quack, but an extraordinary rhythm cooing, that sounds like a cartoon version of a shocked old lady: 'Ooo, ooo, ooo.' Try it out loud, making the middle 'ooo' go up in pitch, and you'll get the idea – a bit like a Frankie Howerd impression! As if the call isn't showy enough, the Eider Drakes are about as conspicuous as a bird can get, being brilliant contrasted black and white. The females, on the other hand, are as drab as the brown seaweed they often sit amongst. At first glance, you might assume they are on nests, but they're not. In fact, the Eiders nest way up amongst grassy tussocks, sometimes well inland, often quite a flight or even a long waddle from the sea.

The lowest actual nesters on the first floor of the rocky high-rise are the Shags. In their breeding plumage they sport extravagant forehead quiffs that Ace Ventura or the lead heart-throb in *Grease* would be proud of. The Shag is also one of those birds for which it is really worth putting the bins – or better still a telescope – on to to appreciate its subleties. Shags may look all black, but the close-up view, especially in sunlight, reveals a glossy-green sheen on their main plumage, a flash of yellow on the beak and a startling pale emerald eye. Another lesson demonstrated: enjoy individual birds as well as the massed ranks.

The ranks don't come much more massed than on the ledges a little higher up the cliff. It is immediately obvious that each species has its own area. One section seems to be entirely Kittiwakes, drawing attention to themselves by relentlessly calling their name. They build rather neat little nests, appropriate to the neatest of all gulls. Early in the season, often both male and female are cuddled up together, maybe mutually preening or even mating. A moment of intimacy amongst the bustle, well worth focusing on and enjoying.

Another section of the cliff belongs to the Guillemots – row upon row of them. They build no nest at all, and they are lined up along a ledge so narrow that it seems a miracle that they don't knock each other off. The fact that they lay eggs along there seems even more miraculous – and possibly foolhardy – until you see that the egg is in the shape of an elongated triangle, designed so that, if it gets a nudge, it simply swivels round on the spot.

The Razorbills use the same principle. They aren't as numerous as the Guillemots, but, once you get used to picking them out by their blacker plumage, there turns out to be more of them than you thought. This part of the colony is the most crowded and conspicuous. There is safety in numbers – the ledges are so densely populated that a predator wouldn't find landing space – and the cliff is a sheer vertical. The birds don't need to hide.

Carrying on up to the next level, however, things become a little more secretive. Here the slope is slightly gentler, and the cliff is more colourful. There are cushions of green grass, studded with patches of pink thrift and white scurvygrass. It is a prettier setting, and it is home to two of the prettiest seabirds. Deep in the shadows of the rocky clefts, the Black Guillemots nest. In even darker dens, a foot or two underground inside old rabbit burrows, the Puffins raise their young. In June, they haven't yet got round to that, though. There may be a few sitting on eggs down there, but the majority seem to be still checking out the holes and one another. Some look as if they haven't got much to do at all, except gather in groups and gossip.

I am always a little loath to bestow human characteristics on birds – 'anthropomorphize' is the big word for it. But in the case of Puffins it's irresistible. When they gather in little groups, they really do look like a reunion of ex-military gents in evening suits, reminiscing before going into dinner. When a bird scuttles along with a beakful of small fish, this even resembles a droopy moustache. Drawing fanciful visual parallels is one thing, but crediting birds with thoughts or emotions is another. In the case of the Puffins, their behaviour was easy enough to translate into purely ornithological terms – they were forming pair bonds, investigating nest sites, performing display rituals, and so on – but the behaviour of the Fulmars I found rather less easy to interpret.

Fulmars are the nearest we have to Albatrosses. They are much smaller – not much bigger than, say, the familiar Black-headed Gulls – but they do display several characteristics similar to those of their much bigger ocean-going Southern hemisphere cousins. Like the Albatrosses, Fulmars have tube noses – a small filter on top of the beak to sift out the salt from seawater – and they have stiff, glider-like wings that make them true masters of the air. It was this flight that captivated and puzzled me as I lay on the clifftop. There were about a dozen of them, putting on an aerobatic display I shall never forget. At first I simply admired and enjoyed them. Then I tried to focus on just one or two individual birds and work out what was the actual purpose of their activities. Well, they weren't catching food, that was for sure, since Fulmars feed

The common British Auks: Puffin, Razorbill and Guillemot.

Fulmar – the joy of flying.

down below off the surface of the sea. They weren't coming into their nesting-ledges either. There were a few birds doing that, but they simply flew in, landed rather clumsily, and shuffled on to their single white eggs. No, the birds I was fixed on were in constant motion. Sometimes they would simply glide along the top of the cliff, at my eye-level, almost brushing my binoculars with their wing-tips. Then they would circle round and zoom straight at the rock-face, stalling only at the last minute, and banking away into the blue. At other times they would hang on the up-draughts, almost hovering like Kestrels over a motorway, but also rising and falling, as if they were dangling from invisible elastic threads. Time and again, they would repeat these actions, sometimes in sequence, sometimes varying their manoeuvres: never landing, never panicking, always completely in control, riding the wind. If they had been planes at an air show, I would have said they were putting on a show for me and the other spectators. Although I was sure the Fulmars were not doing it to please an audience, I did wonder if they were doing it to please themselves. After watching them for nearly an hour, I could come to no other conclusion than that they were revelling in their own expertise, having fun, exhilarated by the joy of flying. I certainly envied them.

So, it seemed, did some of the Puffins. Unfortunately, Puffins are not quite so agile in the air. A couple of them appeared to try to emulate the Fulmar's near-kamikaze zoom-and-stall trick, but only ended up by crash-landing on the clifftop and tumbling beak over tail. There was also a lovely moment when a single Puffin broke away from a little group and marched to the edge of the precipice, as if inviting the others to watch. This they duly did, for all the world like a bunch of admiring teenagers about to witness the gang leader attempt a particularly impressive dare.

The show-off paused, and momentarily glanced back to make sure he had their attention. 'OK, lads, just watch this. I'll show those uppity Fulmars. I can outfly the lot of 'em.'

'Go on, then,' urged the group.

'OK, I will.'

'So go on, then.'

'In a second. Just waiting for the right up-draught.' Still he hesitated. Then he raised his wings. 'Right, then… '

He held this pose for fully a minute. I almost expected his chums to break into a slow hand-clap. Feeling the pressure of expectation, he leaned forward and gave a couple of practice flaps. We all watched.

'OK. Here I go. Ready for take-off. Three… two… one… '

And then, just as we were all about to gasp in admiration, instead of launching himself into the blue… he turned and scuttled back down a rabbit burrow! Puffin? Chicken, more like!

He shouldn't have felt embarrassed, he'd given me the best laugh I'd had for days.

The next day, and on many other days over the years, I have returned to the clifftops with my camera to try to record some of the atmosphere and action. But – like I said – no picture can match the real thing.

Seabird colonies are quite simply terrific entertainment. I have enjoyed their magic right across the world, from the Galapagos to the Seychelles. Nevertheless, I can honestly say that we have the best in Britain, and you don't have to go to Fair Isle to experience the excitement. Hermaness in Shetland, the Farnes in Northumberland, Bempton in Yorkshire, Skomer and Skokholm in Pembrokeshire, and others are all brilliant. What's more, I really don't think you have to be a committed birdwatcher to appreciate them. I have seen children and holidaymakers equally captivated. Whenever anyone asks me what is the appeal of birdwatching, I always wish I could instantly transport them to a seabird colony for an hour or two. I defy them not to enjoy themselves.

DEEDS OF DARKNESS

There were other aspects of my Fair Isle visits whose appeal was perhaps not quite so universal as the scenery and the seabirds. I have already mentioned the trapping and ringing. The very fact that qualification and a licence is necessary in order for people to handle birds, means that many visitors to the Observatory are excluded from these activities. They can still enjoy seeing birds in the hand, and indeed they may well be invited to help driving the traps, but there are certain things that have to be left to those with the proper training. Mind you, some of those things only the intrepid – or indeed slightly deranged – would want to attempt.

For example, dazzling. Birds, like moths, are attracted to bright lights, especially at night. Not that I truly appreciated just how many species do migrate after dark until one memorable September night spent up Fair Isle's south lighthouse back in the early 1960s. It was moonless, misty and wet; exactly the conditions when the birds are drawn in by the light. So were the birdwatchers. Even the journey down the island was exciting; a white-knuckle ride on the back of a motorbike that would have been a major attraction at Alton Towers. The adrenalin pumped even harder as we scaled the lighthouse stairs and emerged on the balcony. The weather swirled around us. So did the birds. It was, simultaneously, thrilling and slightly disturbing, as ghostly shapes flitted through the beams, some escaping into the gloom, others being lured by the lamp, fluttering frantically against the glass. Wheatears, pipits, warblers; we caught so many we had to take our socks off and use them as emergency bird bags! It might well have been a bit whiffy in there, but I suppose they were the lucky ones, as we found several sad little corpses under the light in the morning. The next time I went to the island, the lighthouse had been floodlit and, though I was happy for the birds, I can't pretend I wasn't a little disappointed.

It was on this visit, however, that I discovered dazzling. For a combi-nation of mystery and excitement (and a good laugh), there is nothing to beat it! The principle is basically the same as when rabbits get caught in a car's headlamps. The animals are mesmerized, some of them to such an extent that, instead of carrying on crossing the road, they sit and wait to be mowed down, unless the sympathetic motorist spots them, stops and encourages them to get out of danger. Even then, it is likely that he may have to turn his lights off before the rabbit will come out of its trance, back to its senses, and hop off. The same thing can happen with birds. Nightjars have a habit of sitting on roads in warm climes such as Africa or the Caribbean, and they too get dazzled by car lights. It doesn't happen much in Britain though, mainly because we have very few Nightjars (not because they have been run over, but because their heathland habitat is constantly being depleted). Neither does it happen much on Fair Isle, which only has one road anyway. Nevertheless, there are birds out there waiting to be dazzled. The problem is finding them.

It is quite a big island anyway, and the task isn't made any easier by the fact that the ideal dazzling conditions are much the same as at the lighthouse. The lousier the weather, the better. For a start, this forces the birds to fly low and even seek shelter by landing. Of course, the murk means that you can't see them, but it also means that they can't see you, which is the second advantage of a dirty night. In theory, you should be able to approach the birds without scaring them away. Then, if you can find them with the beam of your flashlight, you should be able to transfix them to the spot – just like those rabbits – so that you can actually catch them by hand and take them back for ringing. It may seem rather a disrupting experience for a migrant, but in fact the bird ends up spending a relatively comfortable night in a nice snug ringing-room roosting-box, rather than being buffeted by a gale and soaked by rain. The next morning, it is released to carry on its migration, bearing a shiny new ring as a testament to its contribution to the science of ornithology. It is certainly none the worse for its experience. In any case, one thing is for sure: on a dazzling expedition, it is the ringers who are likely to suffer the greatest indignities.

We certainly did. It was a thoroughly foul October night when a bold but barely competent trio set out, after a rather too hearty evening meal at the Obs. There was me, the qualified ringer, Andrew, an old birding chum and the daddy of all twitchers, Ron Johns. Ron may be deadly serious in pursuit of a 'tick', but he is an equally avid seeker of a silly experience. He was not to be disappointed.

We were fully armed with a big butterfly net and a couple of strong torches but, so utterly black was the night, we could hardly see our own feet, let alone any birds. Nevertheless, we successfully dazzled three sheep, a large rock and a gate post before realizing that we were totally lost. In fact, we had wandered into a particularly treacherous marshy area that we would not normally have attempted to cross during daylight, let alone in pitch-darkness.

We should have panicked. Instead, we were reduced to helpless laughter. Andrew was the first to go, getting hysterical as he lost his wellies in the mud. I attempted to rescue him with the butterfly net, but only succeeded in tripping over a submerged stone, losing control of my balance and my bodily functions. My shock expressed itself in the form of a loud fart. At this Ron, who was, rather smugly, just about to reach dry land, turned to make a ribald remark, stepped straight into a four-foot ditch and completely disappeared. It was a moment worthy of *Carry On Birding!* We crawled home, bruised, soaked to the skin and in fits of uncontrollable giggles. A small flock of passing Redwings must have heard us. Half a dozen of them suddenly appeared out of the blackness and plummeted down towards our torches. Amazingly, they actually settled on the heather, stared impassively at us and allowed us to net them gently and pop them into bags. Proof indeed: dazzling really did work. Or had they just felt sorry for us? In any event, it was a satisfying climax to an unforgettable night.

The next day was pretty memorable too: the island was alive with thousands of winter thrushes. It was one of those 'falls' that a birdwatcher dreams about. It was impressive indeed, but not as truly fantastic as May 1970.

THE GREAT FALL

For me, there is nothing – absolutely nothing – as thrilling as witnessing a really big fall of migrants. In 1970, between May 7th and 11th, Fair Isle enjoyed one of the most spectacular falls in its history. I enjoyed it too. I was there. Lucky me!

The effect of weather on birds is a complicated affair, but sometimes it is possible to predict, or at least hope. The situation developing during the first week of May 1970 certainly looked promising. An anticyclone (an area of high pressure) had appeared over the Low Countries (Belgium,

Holland, etc.) and then moved north, establishing itself over Scandinavia. The significance of this was that it would have provided clear skies and starry nights, ideal flying and navigating conditions for migrant birds travelling to their breeding grounds. The normal route is up the eastern side of the North Sea – in other words not over Britain – but this weather pattern had also brought with it a brisk easterly wind. Chances were, then, that the stream of birds might well be pushed across the sea towards our coasts. This gave us cause for optimism. However, the flaw in the theory was that the weather was so pleasant that the migrants might simply carry on flying, without any need to land, until they reached their North European destinations. Normally a 'fall' only occurs when the birds hit a patch of nasty weather and are disoriented and forced down. By May 7th, the wind on Fair Isle had been from the south-east for several days, but no significant arrival of migrants had occurred. Our disappointment was no doubt caused – but also alleviated – by the fact that the weather was glorious, sunny and mild. We wandered round the relatively birdless island in T-shirts, at a time of the year when Shetland often demands woolly jumpers and fleece-lined anoraks. Our feelings were mixed. We welcomed the lovely weather, but we were getting desperate for birds.

Amazingly, we were soon enjoying both. The key factor was a depression (low pressure), with its attendant mist and rain, which must have caught the migrants by surprise as they streamed over the North Sea somewhere parallel with Scotland. By the time they emerged from out of the storm, they were wet and weary, and anxious to find land. What they found was Shetland in general, and Fair Isle in particular. Both were still bathed in sunshine; as indeed were we birdwatchers. The first sign that something special was about to happen was the appearance of a Black-headed Wagtail. Theoretically, this is only a 'race' of the common Yellow Wagtail, but it has two major things going for it. First, it is a very beautiful bird. The black head is as glossy as silk and the contrast with an olive-green back and dazzling lemon-coloured underparts is absolutely stunning. Second, the Black-headed Wagtail does not belong in Britain, but

Black-headed Wagtail. Not a 'real' species – but well worth seeing.

hails from south-eastern Europe. Its appearance was a clear indication that we could expect migrants from some way away, and they would no doubt include more scarce species.

There were hardly more than a dozen of us on the island: the warden, two assistants, and a gaggle of visitors. At such times there suddenly seems an awful lot of ground to cover. The appropriate technique is to split up and deploy forces to all parts, but inevitably this is a slightly nerve-racking process. Some parts are better than others and, though everyone tries to keep in touch, it is perfectly possible to miss good birds if you are in the wrong place at the wrong time. Nowadays, mobile phones and a Land Rover, which tours the island brandishing a red flag when a rarity has been sighted, make it far less likely that anyone will 'dip out' (twitcher's parlance for missing a rarity). However, back in May 1970, we had to rely on good luck and take a few risks.

I took the biggest risk of all. Most of the cover on the island is amongst the crofts and crops down in the south. I went north. By the time the sun began to set, I had seen very little and was beginning to think I had chosen the wrong option. Weary and rather disappointed, I slumped down on the clifftop near the North Light and started nibbling a consoling Mars Bar. As I gazed down at the beach below, my eyes began to focus. It was as if the cliffs were coming to life. A Redstart flicked down on to the seaweed. Every damp patch had a Willow Warbler on it. Clearly birds were arriving, 'hitting' the cliff and slowly working their way upwards. Suddenly, hardly a yard away from me, two Bluethroats popped over the crest, their red, white and blue breasts looking for all the world like Union Jacks they were about to plant at the summit. I almost cheered. I had a feeling that the next day was going to be pretty amazing.

It was. Not least because the weather continued to be clear and dry – on Fair Isle, at any rate. Meanwhile, further south, the fog and drizzle continued to do its job. On the island, it rained birds. What's more, the deluge continued for two or three days. The figures conjure up some of the picture. Wheatears:

Bluethroat, complete with Union Jack waistcoat.

2000 on the 8th, rising to 4000 on the 9th. Redstarts: 300 on the the 8th, 700 on the 9th. Whinchats: 350. At least 1000 Willow Warblers, 500 Tree Pipits, 120 Pied Flycatchers and – more exotic and therefore even more exciting species – 35 Wrynecks, 14 Red-backed Shrikes, 10 Ortolan Buntings and no fewer than 35 Bluethroats.

But, in truth, it isn't the statistics that stick in the memory so much as certain images and incidents. I shall never forget looking up as a cascade of Tree Pipits plummeted down so abruptly that I instinctively ducked. Or the afternoon that I tramped across to the west cliffs. At first I thought I had drawn the short straw when I volunteered to trek across the moor to an area that was usually bleak and unproductive. My feet were blistered and my ankles aching by the time I staggered down on to the green sward on the far side of the island. The grass was very short over there, cropped to golf-course standard by the sheep. There was absolutely no other vegetation at all. It was about the last place you'd expect to find Willow Warblers. And yet there they were, in their hundreds, hopping around in a moving carpet so dense that I had to be careful where I trod. I decided the safest policy was to sit down. Even then, it seemed I constituted a danger: I nearly sat on a Corncrake! The poor bird shot out from behind the small rock I had chosen as a stool, and flapped away like a demented chicken. I could hardly blame it. It would have been an ironical fate indeed had it survived a flight of several thousand miles across sand, sea and storm, only to end up being squashed by a birder's bum. It did, however, provide me with a wonderful view of the bird in flight: the first – and still the only – time I have seen a Corncrake completely out in the open. They were not common birds back then. Nowadays, they have been reduced to a few pairs breeding in the Western Isles and in Ireland, and they are severely threatened all across Europe. Imagine the guilt if I had hastened their possible extinction by sitting on that one!

As well as the commoner migrants, which also included such oddities as a Great Spotted Woodpecker, frantically looking for non-existent trees, there were, as we had hoped, several real rarities. As is often the case, the majority of these were found on the days just after the main fall. Presumably this was partly because it was only then that we had time to search properly, after the hectic activities of counting, trapping and ringing. Also, there were fewer birds to search through. By the 11th, the numbers had definitely dwindled. Nevertheless, it was that day that provided us with two truly memorable and rather bizarre incidents.

First, there was the Thrush Nightingale chase. The species is appropriately named. Basically, it looks like a common Nightingale, but it does have a slightly speckled breast. It is also a genuinely rare bird, made all the more desirable by the fact that it generally skulks under cover and tries hard not to be seen. Of course, this tactic is not quite so easy to pursue on Fair Isle, especially in spring when the crops have hardly begun to sprout. In fact, we had already recorded two Thrush Nightingales that week. The one on the 8th had tried to be true to type by scuttling under a rhubarb patch, but the next one – on the 9th – I myself had found resting in the midday sun by a sheltered geo. Both of us, that is: me and the bird.

The third – on the 11th – I actually caught. Well, sort of. It had spent the morning leading the Observatory staff a merry dance round a large field, which was gradually becoming surrounded on all sides by walls of mist-nets. (These large panels of fine mesh, stretched between bamboo poles, are the most frequent and efficient method of catching small birds.) However, just as the Warden had his back turned tying off the last pole, the bird made a bid for freedom, zooming past him and diving into the safety of some derelict farm buildings. Or so it thought. It landed on the doorstep of an old barn, heaved a sigh of relief, and turned back to laugh at its would-be captors. At which point... I ran fifty yards straight at it, waving my arms and pishing wildly like an incensed tom-cat. Understandably, the bird turned tail and flew into the barn, where it took a sharp left and flattened itself against a window, thus temporarily knocking itself out. Happily, it soon recovered and was sent on its way, bearing a shiny new ring, and with a story to tell its mates when it finally reached Sweden or wherever it was bound for.

If the chase for the Thrush Nightingale required a burst of energy, the Crake required a great deal of faith and patience. The sequence of events began early in the morning, when the Warden, returning from his trap round, thought he spotted a small

Thrush Nightingale in its natural habitat — a rhubarb patch.

bird scurrying up a drain-pipe! What sounded like an hallucination seemed less fanciful when we actually visited the site later in the day. It was close to the Plantation. At this point a stream crosses under the road and flows through a section of piping to aid its progress, directing it out on to the boggy moorland. It was here that, while driving the Plantation trap, the Warden had caught a movement out of the corner of his eye. It was so subliminal that he really couldn't be sure if it was a rodent or a bird. Peering through the pipe produced neither. But the nagging doubt remained, which explained why, at midday, half a dozen of us could be seen crawling around on our hands and knees by the side of the road, making sure that there really was nothing lurking underneath it. We were just on the point of finally accepting that there wasn't, when someone yelled, 'There it is.' To which the immediate response was: 'Where?' and 'What?'

The answer to 'Where?' was: 'Halfway up the stream, out in the moor.' The answer to 'What?' was: 'A small Crake.'

Crakes are the family name for the group of gangly-legged birds that include the familiar Moorhen. Most of them live in damp places, except the Corncrake which, as its name implies, prefers crops. Even a Moorhen would have been an unusual occurrence on Fair Isle, but a 'small Crake' had to be something really good.

The problem is that the smaller and rarer the Crake, the more skulking its behaviour is likely to be. There are some species, in some parts of the world, that live in the depths of impenetrable reed-beds and are heard but are seen so rarely that people begin to wonder if they actually exist! However, there are no dense reed-beds on Fair Isle. In fact, it seemed as if our party of birdwatchers, few though we were, had surely got the mystery bird surrounded. It had disappeared under the overhanging bank of the narrow stream that crossed the moor. The person who had glimpsed it pinpointed the spot, and we split up either side of it. Then we began walking towards each other, gently chivvying along the stream, confident that the bird would pop out and reveal its identity. Two minutes later we met in the middle. We had seen nothing. It couldn't have flown off. It had to still be in there. We repeated the manoeuvre. Still nothing. Had the Crake crawled under the bank and died? Or had it dug an escape tunnel? We were just about to give up, when I caught the sort of glimpse the Warden must have had earlier in the day.

'There!' I yelled. But no one else had seen it.

'What was it?'

'I don't know,' I replied. 'It is a Crake, and it is very small. About the size of a Starling.'

'Could it be a Starling?' someone asked sceptically.

'Well, I suppose so,' I muttered, suddenly taken with the sort of cautionary nervousness that birdwatchers sometimes experience when they think – or hope – they are on the brink of clinching a rarity. Even then, though, I knew it was quite beyond the wiles of even the shyest or most perverse of Starlings to hide for nearly an hour under the bank of a two-foot-wide stream!

No, it was not a Starling, it was definitely a small Crake, and this time I had seen exactly where it had gone in. I walked over and nudged the bank with my foot. Nothing. The Warden gave me a look that expressed something between pity and exasperation, but his attention was suddenly distracted. He motioned for everyone to be quiet and stop all movement. Slowly, he tiptoed along the stream, several yards away from where I was convinced the bird must be. Then he stopped, 'shushed' us again, slowly sank to his knees, and reached under the bank. After five seconds that felt like a minute, he smiled and pulled out his hand. In it he was holding an aptly named Little Crake, at that time only the fifth ever recorded north of the border. Amazingly, an hour later, a rather less rare, but still much appreciated, Spotted Crake was caught in the same ditch. To complete the set, a single Moorhen was also seen and – along with a lone Coot and another Corncrake – this added up to a five-Crake day on Fair Isle.

The whole week added up to one of the most enjoyable birdwatching holidays I have ever had.

| Little Crake. | Spotted Crake. | Corncrake. |

FINAL THOUGHTS: IN PRAISE OF BIRD OBSERVATORIES

I have dwelt so long on my Fair Isle experiences in order not to make you envious but to inspire you. You may fancy visiting the Magic Isle yourself. I would certainly recommend it. As I have already said, you will be able to get there fairly easily, but – alas – you will find the plane fares pretty steep. This is perhaps one of the reasons why when a friend of mine stayed at the Observatory during the first week of October 1995, he had the place almost to himself. Actually, I rather envied him, but it is also a great pity that this wonderful place is so expensive to get to. The second reason Fair Isle – and indeed other Observatories – are sometimes lacking in visitors is the modern-day obsession with twitching. The insatiable pursuit of rarities and long lists means that fewer birdwatchers these days seem prepared to actually stay in one place for long. Many of them prefer to follow the call of birdlines, pagers and mobile phones, and travel wherever the birds may lead them. I have nothing against this – each to his or her own, as they say – but it surely isn't the way to enjoy the atmosphere and ambience of a location, and, in the case of Fair Isle, that seems to me a considerable waste.

Maybe I am nostalgic for the 'good old days', but I really do have a great fondness for Bird Observatories. Fair Isle isn't the only one. There's North Ronaldsay and Stronsay in Orkney; Skokholm and Bardsey in Wales; Spurn in Yorkshire; Portland in Dorset; Sandwich Bay and Dungeness in Kent; Cape Clear in Ireland, and a few others. Accommodation varies, it is true, and some are along fairly basic hostel lines, but if you require a little extra comfort, you could stay in a nearby hotel, boarding-house or rented cottage, whilst continuing to make the Observatory area your daily birding territory. This is, in fact, a way of making any bird holiday more satisfying. Wherever you choose to go, define an area that you cover thoroughly each day, record everything you see and keep a log-book. This way you set up your very own temporary bird observatory, as it were. You might not experience anything quite as spectacular as one of those Fair Isle falls, but you never know!

10 Birding Abroad

I didn't want to go to Disney World. I had troubling visions of raving claustrophobia and total artificiality: wall-to-wall cartoon characters, incessant noise, and thousands of people. Certainly no birds. But it was Laura (my wife) and Rosie (my

Official birding uniform for Disney World.

daughter)'s turn to choose the holiday. So to Walt Disney World we went. It was great.

The flight to Florida was about ten hours. It took almost as long to get our luggage, pass through customs and pick up our hire car. By the time we were on the highway heading west, it was pitch-dark. As we turned off towards the Magic Kingdom, we could see the distant turrets of Cinderella's castle lit up by a massive firework display, whilst closer to us, above somewhere named – rather lasciviously, I thought – Pleasure Island, the sky was lacerated by lasers. Rosie would have liked that, but she was fast asleep in the back of the car. Laura was visibly excited, but she too was feeling pretty weary. I was relieved. We definitely would *not* be going exploring that night. Instead, we checked in at reception and were guided towards our villa, by a man who drove a small motorized trolley and smiled a lot. I was pleased to note that where we were staying wasn't actually surrounded by merry-go-rounds, all-night hamburger stalls or floodlights. In fact, it felt pleasantly peaceful and reassuringly dark. Those certainly looked like real trees we had parked by, and that was surely water that the fireworks were reflected in. Maybe there was a small pond in front of our villa. So far, not as bad as I'd feared.

Nevertheless, as I lay in bed that night, I felt nervous, as I always do at the start of family holidays. It's not that I don't enjoy doing the traditional activities with Laura and Rosie – though I was a little sceptical about the promised pleasures of queueing for two hours to be sick on Space Mountain – but I really can't be happy if birds aren't involved some-where. I don't ask much. Just a few interesting species, and a few hours to watch them. I don't need to disappear for days on end, just for the odd mornings and evenings. The rest of the day is family time, and I am very happy with that. But if there are no birds at all, then I'm not happy. And if I'm not happy, it shows. And then nobody's happy. So, all in all, it's best – for all of us – if wherever we choose for a holiday is not entirely birdless. So what about Disney World then? Laura and Rosie had both chosen it. Surely they wouldn't risk my spoiling it for them? Maybe they had done some research first? I fell asleep mulling over such thoughts, and wondering what it was going to be like out there in the morning.

About six hours later I woke up and panicked. I could hear birdsong. Lots of it. But I had absolutely no idea what any of the birds were. This, to me, is always the most unnerving aspect of being abroad. In Britain, I recognize just about every sound in the dawn chorus. Even in Europe, with a bit of luck, there will be familiar songs to latch on to. But on a different continent, everything is mystery and confusion. What should be sweet music becomes a cacophony. What's more, almost as if to tease you deliberately, there may be songs that sound like British birds, but definitely aren't.

For example, at that very moment, I could hear what sounded like a Blackbird singing just oustide the window. But I knew there weren't any British-type Blackbirds in Florida. There *are* birds that Americans call 'Blackbirds', but they are not thrushes like ours. On the other hand, there *are* American thrushes, but they are tiny. Whatever was singing sounded really big and fruity. Then I thought, 'Maybe it's a Robin.' No, not 'our' Robin, but a big brash Yankee version that is more the size of… yes, a British Blackbird. So was this an American Robin that was mocking me by sounding so familiar?

I sat up in bed and peeped through the curtains. I could see the singer on the nearby roof. I had been closer to guessing right than I'd realized. It wasn't an American Robin. It was a Mockingbird. Good name. It had presumably earned it by driving birdwatchers crazy by impersonating lots of other species. Well, its mimickry was lost on me, since I didn't know what any of them sounded like in the first place! All I knew was that I was feeling confused and not a little edgy. It was the sort of nervousness – mixed with excitement – that a birdwatcher feels when he is stepping into the unknown. As I tiptoed out into the dawn, I formulated my first rule of foreign birding: don't panic! On the first morning, don't worry too much about songs and calls. Try to ignore them until later. Meanwhile, try to find something familiar.

Water is good. For a start, there are some waterbirds that are amazingly and comfortingly ubiquitous. Many species of wader occur almost

Mockingbird – a bird we've all heard of, if not actually heard.

right across the world – Turnstone, Sanderling, Dunlin. And even if the species aren't exactly the same, chances are you will at least recognize the family. Thus, even as I discovered that the pond outside our villa was in fact quite a large lake, I was further encouraged by the sight of what looked like a Moorhen and a Common Sandpiper teetering along the edge. Of course, the birds weren't quite as they seemed. The Sandpiper was in fact a Spotted Sandpiper (the American equivalent, but a different species), whilst the Moorhen was indeed just that, except that they call them Florida Gallinule over there. (Trust the Yanks to nick our birds!) But already I felt calmer. Second rule of foreign birding coming up (and this is the secret of sanity): compare what you see with birds you know from back home.

There, that morning, on that lake, I had an instant opportunity to put the rule into practice. As well as the Sandpiper and the Moorhen, the sunrise lit up a Kingfisher perched on a nearby bridge. Not a tiny British Kingfisher, a huge American one, but recognizably a Kingfisher nevertheless. Fishing out in the middle was what was clearly some kind of Cormorant, whilst wading in the shallows were what were obviously herons, egrets and ibises. One of them looked much like our Grey Heron, but not quite, while another closely resembled a Little Egret. Others were less familiar-looking. There was a small gun-metal-blue

Right Green-backed (or Little Green) Heron.
Below Belted Kingfisher – nice hairdo, huh?

one, and an even tinier one, largely green... and another with at least three colours on it. There were at least two kinds of ibises: a Glossy one – surely the same as the European species – and a white one, no doubt a White Ibis. For about an hour I wandered around looking, enjoying and taking notes.

During breakfast I rummaged through my American field guide, and over coffee I proudly announced to Laura and Rosie that I had seen an amazing twenty-nine species already. They weren't impressed. I offered them Little Blue, Great Blue, Little Green and Tricolored Heron, not to mention Snowy and Great White Egret, Belted Kingfisher and Double-crested Cormorant. But all they wanted was Donald Duck.

During the rest of the week we spent our days exploring Magic Kingdom, Epcot, Sea World and the MGM and Universal Film Studios, and I loved it. I also explored the birds. It did strike me as an extraordinary irony that the only official 'wildlife' attraction at Disney World is a place called Discovery Island, which features tame Parrots and captive Flamingoes, and the like. It is perfectly pretty, but the fact is that there are plenty of wonderful genuinely wild birds to be seen all over the area. There are masses of lakes and masses of waterbirds. I also discovered a variety of waders along the muddier edges and in places where the ground staff had been watering the golf-courses and had thus created temporary marshland. There were birds in the woods – including a splendid variety of dazzlingly coloured American Warblers – and there were birds in the air, including many species of impressive raptor, such as Turkey and Black Vultures, Swallow-tailed Kites and Bald Eagles. I also became familiar with the families we don't get in Britain: the Grackles, Vireos, and so on.

However, this book really isn't the place for an in-depth résumé of American – or indeed Florida – birds. All I want to do is give you a few pointers towards enjoying birds on a family holiday. The first one – and I'm telling myself this too! – is never to assume there there won't be any birds at all. That is almost never true. Of course, some places will be better than others – and, let's face it, Florida really is one of the best – but the principles for maximum value apply more or less universally.

So here's a little list:

• Do some homework first. Buy a field guide that covers the area and – if there is one – a local site guide (a 'where to watch birds in...' book). There happens to be a very good one for Florida.

• Also use your own initiative. As with just about all kinds of birding, the trick is to cover a variety of habitats: wetlands, woods, grassland, mountains, and – if you are near the sea – estuaries, headlands and beaches. Have a good look at the map of the area, and mark likely spots.

• Get out early and late – dawn and dusk – leaving time to enjoy a family holiday as well!

• Negotiate one big day out, when you go off on an expedition to a particularly good site, perhaps at the coast, or a bird reserve. And don't forget to take necessary provisions for braving the elements on your day out, such as sun cream or extra clothing if you're going to a country that is particularly hot or cold.

• If you revisit the same area over the years, try different seasons; that way you'll see different birds.

• And finally (I'll say it again): don't panic! Enjoy!

These principles apply wherever you decide to go – Spain, France, the Balearics, the Canaries, the Caribbean, Africa – though it has to be said that the farther you travel, the less easy it is not to panic when faced with entirely new, completely unfamiliar bird families that bear no resemblance whatsoever to anything we get in Britain. But then, that's part of the fun.

Or you may fancy getting someone else to do some of the work for you, by joining a group on a specialist birding holiday, with an expert guide who will show you the birds and teach you how to identify them. As a matter of fact, I really would recommend this kind of tour. But then I would say that, wouldn't I? Because I occasionally lead them.

Meanwhile, back in Florida... As it has turned out, Laura, Rosie and I have returned to Disney World several times since that first visit. We have been in spring, late summer, autumn and even at Christmas (lucky old us, I'd say). My big days out have included trips to both the Gulf and Atlantic coasts, and to various large lakes and swamps – many of them official Wildife Refuges – all within a couple of hours' drive. The result is that I have seen a lot of beautiful birds. Here are just a few of them...

Left Pileated Woodpecker. Woody's cousin.

Right Cardinal. Typical American show off.

Below right Brown Pelican.

USEFUL ADDRESSES

RSPB (Royal Society for the Protection of Birds)
The Lodge, Sandy,
Bedfordshire,
SG19 2DL
Tel: 01767 680551
Web: www.rspb.org.uk

The RSPB is Britain's leading bird conservation organization, with almost one million members. It runs more than 100 bird reserves, and has a national network of members' groups where you can get to meet other birders. The RSPB has a mail-order service, selling approved nestboxes, bird-feeders and many other items of equipment. Family membership is also available. Members receive four copies of Birds magazine each year; other incentives include a free bird table, or bird identification book or DVD on joining.

BTO (British Trust for Ornithology)
The National Centre for Ornithology,
The Nunnery,
Thetford, Norfolk,
IP24 2PU
Tel: 01842 750050
Web: www.bto.org

The BTO offers birders the opportunity to learn more about birds by taking part in practical projects, such as surveys. These include the Garden BirdWatch, in which people from all over the country record the birds in their garden on a regular basis, and the Nest Record Scheme, participants of which receive a free pack and newsletter. Family membership is also available. Members receive a bi-monthly magazine, BTO News.

The Field Studies Council
Preston Montford, Shrewsbury,
SY4 1HW
Tel: 01743 850674
Web:
www.field-studies-council.org

The Field Studies Council runs eleven centres around England and Wales, where adults and children can take part in day and residential courses on subjects related to the environment and the natural world. Several centres run courses in birdwatching.

The Wildfowl and Wetlands Trust
Slimbridge,
Glos GL2 713T
Tel: 01453 890333
Web: www.wwt.org.uk

The WWT is Britain's leading conservation organization for wildfowl and their habitats. Its headquarters is at Slimbridge, founded by the late Sir Peter Scott. There are seven other centres: four in England and one each in Scotland, Wales and Northern Ireland.

There are many other organizations that may come in useful in the world of birding – a quick internet search should prove a helpful starting point.

FURTHER READING

MAGAZINES

Birdwatch
Birdwatch is the self-styled 'home of birdwatching'. An all-round title, it has news, reviews and articles about the birding world.
Web: www.birdwatch.co.uk

BBC Wildlife Magazine
BBC's magazine covering all things wildlife, including birds from around the world.
Web: bbcwildlifemagazine.com

Bird Watching
Britain's best-selling bird magazine, this is another source of birding news and events, as well as kit tests and reviews.
Web: www.birdwatching.co.uk

Birding World
Monthly magazine for keen birdwatchers, with pictures and info about birds across Europe.
Web: www.birdingworld.co.uk

There are many other birding magazines available, covering a range of areas and levels of expertise. Ask your newsagent or search online for further details.

BOOKS

Birds Britannica
by Mark Cocker and Richard Mabey
(Chatto & Windus, 2005)

Birdscapes: Birds in our Imagination and Experience
by Jeremy Mynott
(Princeton University Press, 2009)

Collins Field Guide to Bird Songs and Calls
by Geoff Sample
(Collins, 1996)

RSPB Handbook of British Birds
by Holden & Cleeves
(Helm, 2010)

RSPB Pocket Guide to British Birds
by Harrap & Nurney
(Helm, 2007)

The Running Sky
by Tim Dee
(Jonathan Cape, 2009)

The Secret Lives of British Birds
by Couzens and Partington
(Helm, 2006)

The Wisdom of Birds
by Tim Birkhead
(Bloomsbury, 2008)

The Secret Lives of British Birds
by Couzens and Partington
(Helm, 2006)

Also by Bill Oddie

Bill Oddie's Gone Birding
(Methuen, 1983)

Follow That Bird
(Robson Books, 1994)

Bill Oddie's Little Black Bird Book (Robson Books, 1995)

Bird in the Nest
(Robson Books, 1995)

Bill Oddie's Gripping Yarns: Tales of Birds and Birding
(Christopher Helm Publishers Ltd, 2000)

One Flew into the Cuckoo's Egg
(Hodder & Stoughton, 2008)

The Running Sky
by Tim Dee
(Jonathan Cape, 2009)

Also by Stephen Moss

**This Birding Life: The Best of
the Guardian's Birdwatch**
(Aurum Press Ltd, 2006)

**A Sky Full of Starlings: A
Diary of a Birding year**
(Aurum Press Ltd, 2008)

The Bumper Book of Nature
(Square Peg, 2009)

There are many other birding books available, ranging from general reference titles to specific field guides. You can find plenty of titles on the internet, or ask your local bookseller for more information.

INDEX